this is mental illness

this is mental illness

HOW IT FEELS
AND WHAT IT MEANS

by Vernon W. Grant, Ph.D.
clinical psychologist

preface by Leston L. Havens, M.D.

beacon press   boston

preface

This book sets out to make psychosis understandable, and
succeeds. Hitherto, novels, plays and an occasional autobiog-
raphy have been the chief popular introductions to "madness,"
and as a result psychosis—or what is coming to be called "major
mental" illness—has remained a distant territory, thickly settled,
but as a rule visited only by those who had to go. Dr. Grant
moves our understanding a long way into the territory, with the
probable result that popular usage and observation will be considerably enriched.

Neurosis has been popularized. In fact, if it is popularized
much more it will become a badge of respectability. Nothing
even remotely like this is true of psychosis. Once recognized,
psychotic symptoms set their victims immediately apart. Hallucinations, delusions, remoteness or inappropriateness of feeling
have a deeply disturbing effect on those brought face to face
with them. Most of us make powerful efforts to *isolate* madness
by calling it names, by heartily signing ourselves up for the conventional and "normal," and by very effectively standing aside
while society arranges the distant rural sequestration of the
severely mentally ill. In Samuel Butler's *Erewhon* the sick went
to jail and the criminals to hospital beds. In our world many of
the mentally sick go to hospitals that are little different from
jails and many that are not so well staffed or equipped as some
jails. This is not an accident. It is one of our methods of putting
the mentally ill *away*. The psychological equivalent of this sequestration is what we call "defenses": those processes which
organize primordial mental life, transform its tendencies, and
which result in the adaptation—or what used to be called the
civilization—of man. Dr. Grant indicates that mental illness

involves not only the breakdown of these "normal" defenses, but also the emergence of new ones, queer, crazy or dangerous to our waking eye. (The dreaming eye is more tolerant.) I think the careful reader of this book will finish it with less need to use such epithets and less need to put the severely mentally ill so far away.

The book presents powerful tools for understanding the oddest happenings of which the human mind is capable as well as persuasive reasons for attempting that understanding. The most persuasive of these is that the author has himself done it. He is no armchair explorer inviting his listeners to venture up these Amazons of the heart and mind while he relaxes in an academic armchair. He has lived and felt with the sickest people that psychological medicine admits. Those who have known similar patients will sense without hesitation the soundness of his observations.

The author gives another reason for reaching out to psychotic people. He tells us not only that he has learned to know and like them; he has also been able to help them. Far from sequestering the mentally ill, he has helped break down their isolation. In doing this he has struck a blow at one of the most tragic facts about psychosis. The psychotic person is "difficult." Society quite naturally withdraws. *And then the psychotic person becomes still more difficult.* The existence of this vicious circle has led many experienced people to believe that society's typical response to the psychotic person is one important cause of *chronic* psychoses, those major mental illnesses which stay major or get worse.

Anyone with mentally sick friends and relatives, anyone whose own mental processes have occasionally brought him or her up short, will find something of interest here—and anyone for whom human psychological processes are a source of excitement and speculation. Modern man has almost explored the surface of his planet. True, the bottom of many seas and a few great inland stretches remain unmapped, but on the terrestrial globe we are like the tidy housewife who fusses to be sure that no corners are uncleaned. In two new areas, however, the unknown vastly surpasses the known, and into each of these the boldest temperaments of the present century have set foot. We have recently begun to reach for the moon and the stars; we have also begun to search the dark and often forbidding inner regions of the mind. It is true that the nineteenth century set its telescopes to the sky and charted the heavenly bodies and their movements. The same was true for the nineteenth-century students of abnormal psychology; they, too, studied the appearance and movement of their subjects, but from a distance, as through a glass darkly. It remained for Freud, Meyer and Sullivan, to name only the most celebrated, to *enter* the unknown territory and bring back from it new knowledge and understanding.

In taking up this book you are not, however, putting yourself in the hands of an adventurer or conquistador. The author is truly a guide, and like a good guide, he has made the unfamiliar and exotic not romantic or mysterious but *familiar;* in fact, he has linked the unfamiliar with the most everyday. The guide takes us step by step where we are going, free of anxiety or bewilderment. He lets us feel the links to home, in this case the links to our most familiar, and sometimes not so familiar, selves. So gentle has he made the journey, one may sometimes wonder if we have ventured away from home at all, until we look back and remember where we have been.

The writer of this introduction has no wish to be a niggardly host and subject the reader in advance to academic or scientific reservations he may have. For the most part, these are minor. Our understanding of psychosis is not so large that any viewpoint would satisfy everyone. In fact, there is only one large matter for which I would take the author to task. He comes down very hard on parents. This is in the air nowadays and no doubt with good reason. He could, in fact, have cited several recent investigations, notably those of Hill, Lidz and Bateson, to make more specific what *is* the matter between parents and children who develop schizophrenia. But, in Al Smith's words, all the returns aren't in. Many of the psychological and physiological characteristics that climax in a psychosis may well have their beginnings outside the early home life, in genetic features that go back many generations, or in intrinsic or adaptive difficulties of an altogether different kind. As Erik Erikson has written of childhood schizophrenia, we can never be sure whether what he terms the "failure of sending power" is first in the mother or in the child.

Otherwise he seems to me "fair" in an area so provocative of feelings of guilt and blame (not only on the part of lay people but among doctors and scientists, too) that it is very hard indeed to be fair.

Those interested in the *physical* causes or concomitants of mental disease get short shrift here and will need to look elsewhere. But this is for a good reason. The author has tried to stay close to his experience, and his experience has been with the psychological and social sources of major mental illness.

From the historical point of view the book is part of a large movement, long overdue in this country and abroad, to admit the mentally ill to society. It began with Pinel, Tuke, Chiarugi and a few others at the time of the French Revolution, was interrupted through much of the nineteenth century and has only gathered significant momentum in recent years. The unlocking of mental hospital doors, the employment of the mentally ill in industry, the growing recognition of the enormous impact of emotional distress on every phase of life, are merely the best known signs that a great minority, among us and in each of us, is being desegregated. Dr. Grant's book is a sign of the change, and a reason it will progress further.

Do not, however, expect Dr. Grant to cure anyone's schizophrenia or make the patient be glad he's psychotic. The author has told us some of the reasons why many people have to be very sick; he does not pretend to know them all. Nor does he make the experience of being psychotic a bland or cheerful one. But he does make it more understandable.

Leston L. Havens, M.D.

*To the patients: that society may be helped
to better understand them.*

contents

introduction:

schizophrenics are people

During eight years of work in a mental hospital, I have spent a large part of each day talking to schizophrenics, observing and studying them. Altogether, I have probably spent more time with schizophrenics during these years than with normal people. I have had schizophrenic typists and even a schizophrenic secretary. Often, apart from my duties, I have spent an hour with one of these people for the sheer pleasure of his society. I have known schizophrenics with exceptionally high IQ's, and some who once held jobs with considerable responsibility. I have found most schizophrenics likable.

Although from a few I was separated by a gulf of silence, or of suspicion and evasiveness, or by phrases I could not understand, with the vast majority I was able to carry on a quite intelligible conversation. Most of them could easily pass, unrecognizable in appearance and manner, in a mentally normal group. No more than a very few would attract attention by a curious gesture, by a fixed gaze, by a certain lack of expression, or by speech directed, apparently, to no one in particular.

Delusional patients have fitted me into their systems of persecution and have seen me as an enemy, a secret Communist, an undercover agent or as a special protector. Patients who heard "voices" have heard my own voice, among others. I have figured as the guilty party in a hallucinated murder, in fantasied sexual assaults and erotic advances. I confused one patient by having several "doubles" who from time to time replaced me in her perceptions.

Some of these people were hostile, at least at first, and a few remained so to the end of my contacts. Yet never did I feel that this hostility was directed toward me in any personal sense. It was always, rather, something the patient brought with him "out of life," that is, life outside the hospital. It was rooted somewhere in the past, a hatred or a resentment still simmering from old offenses and old hurts. More important, it seemed never more than a surface emotion, however persistent. The essential person "beneath" was friendly, with as much latent kindliness as anyone else.

Rarely was there one of whom I could not feel that, behind the barrier of unbroken silence or the facade of dreamy detachment or suspicious withdrawal or even of cold rejection, there was somewhere an altogether human and understandable personality. It was always possible to believe that for all the distorted and at times very "queer" modes of thinking the underlying emotions and desires were in no way essentially different from those of a normal person. However strange or unusual the expression might be, the *feelings*, it seemed to me, must be altogether like my own.

I have but one single purpose in this book. I want to show that the outwardly strange behavior of the mentally ill not only makes sense in terms of normal human feelings and desires, but that much of it, while seemingly pointless as well as abnormal, actually *serves a purpose*. The symptom may in some way defend against fear, reduce fear, ease a feeling of guilt or protect self-esteem.

"Insanity" is commonly viewed as a major evil, but to understand how it feels and what it means we must first understand that the abnormal symptoms may shield the patient from a distress which might be, for him, a still greater evil than "insanity." This will be illustrated from actual case histories of mental illness, most of them schizophrenia, since that form of major mental illness afflicts at least half of those persons hospitalized for "insanity," psychosis or mental illness. If not all of the cases included would be recognized by a professional psychologist or psychiatrist as schizophrenics, this is in part because single features have often been selected from the larger whole of a case history and focused upon as illustrative of some one aspect of mental illness.*

For a number of reasons, some of which would be meaningful only to those who have worked in state psychiatric hospitals, fully adequate follow-up information on the cases reported in this book was in many instances not available. Some improved with psychotherapy, some did not. Some were released before the studies were completed, and others could not be given adequate treatment during their period of hospitalization. Since this book primarily emphasizes the dynamics and meaning of illness, I feel that discussion of the character and outcome of treatment is not essential.

To say that a mental symptom, such as a delusion, may serve a purpose, may suggest a conscious design on the part of the patient. It suggests something done "on purpose." Here the comparison with such a physical reaction as fever may be helpful. The layman may think of fever as a disorder in the sense of a breakdown of the body machinery that controls temperature. It means something out of order in the sense that a car is out of order when the motor overheats. In the same way, a patient's belief in persecutors, persistently held although highly unreasonable and contradicted by facts, looks like a clear enough sign of defective mental machinery, a mind out of order.

But a physician will tell us that the rise of temperature in fever is in reality a natural and useful response of the body to disease. It can similarly be shown that a delusional disorder is likewise a "natural" and useful response of the mind, and also that it is just as little intended by a person under stress of certain kinds of emotional conflicts.

---

* That some cases to be described may not be clearly recognizable as schizophrenics might also be due to the lack of universal agreement as to the definition and characteristics of the disorder.

help person his handle his problems in way that he wishes of The best way and a means of coping

Much of the meaning of mental illness lies in this: that the symptom, though it upsets a person's life and even leads to hospitalization, may yet be, *for him*, the solution to a problem. It serves a need, does some good, in some way makes living better for him than it would otherwise be. That by normal standards the person may be judged ill does not alter the fact that this kind of illness brings rewards.

There is, again, a certain tendency in popular thinking to suppose that mental illness includes something more than the symptoms. Thus a person is said to be doing or saying certain unusual things because he is mentally ill. The illness, supposedly, causes him to act and speak as he does.

"Mental illness" is, first of all, a pair of words. These words are a name for certain ways of thinking, feeling and behaving which differ from what is considered normal. The words are a name for a particular way of reacting to situations. For example, in one of the disorders to be studied, a person mistakenly perceives others as unfriendly or threatening. He is said to have a "persecution complex." One source of this is the habitual feeling of rejection. It would be misleading, however, to say that the abnormal ways of feeling and perceiving are caused by "mental illness." These ways of feeling and perceiving *are* the illness. Too often the term suggests a mysterious something *behind* the unusual behavior.

Not only are schizophrenics people, but it is in relation to other people that in the main their illness shows. It is a disorder of social behavior; it revolves about thoughts and feelings which are responses to others.

A visitor to a psychiatric hospital, viewing an exhibit of handiwork from the occupational or industrial therapy departments, may often remark: "It is hard to believe that people who can do such skilled and complicated work can be mentally disordered." The comment illustrates an important feature of schizophrenic illness, as well as a popular notion about disorders of the mind. It is easy to find a mechanic, for example, who was doing highly competent work at his skilled occupation within a few days of his admission to a hospital, or a secretary who likewise functioned efficiently, so long as she functioned at all, until removal from her job became necessary. The professional artist, the musician or the seamstress may continue to perform impressively well.

It is true that there are periods of this illness during which, owing to confusion, preoccupation or apathy, these skills may operate badly. The patient may be too distracted by his disturbance to use them properly. The point is that the disorder need not affect a person's ability to deal with *things*. Typically it is his social relationships that are disturbed.

Thus, we find that if the mechanic did handle his job less well than usual, it was because he was troubled with anxiety about the seemingly strange behavior of those about him, or because he heard talk that was puzzling or threatening. If the secretary's work was not satisfactory, it was because she had become painfully self-conscious, or suffered from the feeling that she had become unpopular, or perhaps was troubled with the idea that a movement to obtain her dismissal was under way. Again and again we discover, at the beginnings of the illness, that *people,* in the patient's experience, have become apparently unfriendly, or too watchful, or that they seem to behave strangely, and that his disturbed emotions are the consequence of these actions of others.

A great psychiatrist has said that "there is nothing unique in the phenomena of the gravest mental illness. The most peculiar behavior of the acutely schizophrenic patient . . . is made up of interpersonal processes with which each one of us is or . . . has been familiar. For the greater part of the performance . . . of the psychotic patient is exactly of a piece with processes which we manifest some time every twenty-four hours." [1]

A chief stimulus to the writing of this book was the almost daily encounter with evidence, in the behavior of schizophrenic patients, of clear likenesses to various features of normal mental life. Repeatedly these led to the thought: if these likenesses and their meanings can be explained to the layman, would it not be of value, not only to remove the gap in popular thinking between normality and mental illness, but also to arouse a more sympathetic attitude toward it through better understanding?

One of the commonest marks of schizophrenic thinking, for example, is that it is "out of touch with reality," meaning that among other things it is thinking that does not truthfully or accurately reflect the facts of a situation. Thus, a hospitalized schizophrenic boy planned to obtain money from his father for a lawyer, who was to get release for a hospitalized girl, whom the patient would then marry. While he professed to be somewhat uncertain whether the project could be carried out, it was evident that he was preoccupied with it, and that he saw nothing really impractical about it. Apart from the obvious fact that he had confused a medical matter with a legal one, the facts were that his father would have instantly dismissed the idea as unthinkable, that the girl had shown small interest in him, and that he had been given no grounds for thinking that he was, himself, to be released. The boy was intelligent enough to recognize these facts, and they were available to him, but he had allowed his desires to blind his perceptions. The people concerned were not at all inclined as he supposed them to be. His "plan" was strongly flavored with fantasy.

Again, a very dependent schizophrenic girl, who felt rejected by her family, repeatedly approached people on very short acquaintance with an account of her personal problems, followed with the plea that they take her into their homes and, in effect, make her one of the family. The plea was always refused, often with evidence—or what would have been evidence to another— of puzzled surprise and curiosity. Despite these failures, the girl repeatedly renewed her attempts. She could not see why her request should be regarded as unreasonable. She was not aware of the feelings her advances aroused in others. She did not know why she was refused. She had not learned, it appeared, that "people are not like that."

This behavior was all of a piece with the more obviously delusional symptoms of these patients. Yet it is quite equally all of a piece with many familiar and altogether normal instances in

which thinking follows closely upon desires and leaves realities
well behind. For example, a student of mine was during college
years an enthusiastic socialist, sincerely confident that sweeping
social changes were waiting only upon nationwide public en-
lightenment. This he tried to assist by soap-boxing at every opportunity. He soon abandoned the faith, however, not through
rejection of the doctrines but because of the difficulty of making
converts. People became interested, he found, but other concerns diverted them and the interest languished. The sparks he
kindled seemed genuine, but they soon smoldered. He sensed a
"vast inertia" in the average man. As he put it: "I had the wrong
picture of the way people are, and how much resistance there is
to change. I saw what an enormous job it would be, and how long
it would take. I guess my enthusiasm kept me from realizing it
sooner." He had been, he might have said, out of touch with certain realities of human behavior.

It is my belief that no single task of advancing mental health
is more important than that of public education. The cases to be
described were studied in a state hospital setting. That conditions
in these hospitals may be unfavorable to recovery has been repeatedly stressed by many observers. That lack of public interest
in, and knowledge of, mental illness has much to do with these
conditions has perhaps not been stressed enough. As Dr. W. C.
Menninger has said: "Basically our state hospitals are neglected
because of the widespread fear of mental illness and of those who
are mentally ill. Remaining ignorant and uninformed on this social problem is a protective device against that fear. In the absence of factual information, misconceptions have grown up and
continue to exist about both psychiatry and emotionally ill patients." [2]

The fear of mental illness can be removed only by understanding. The effort must go much further, however, than mere
reassurance. It is not enough to repeat the statement that mental
illness is no sinister loss of human qualities and feelings, that it is,
rather, a change rooted in understandable fears, resentments,
guilt feelings and conflicts. This is true, but this truth must be

shown by way of readable descriptions of these changes, and through meaningful accounts of their origins.

Most people have little or no authentic knowledge of what mental illness is really like. They do not know what the signs of disorder are, not only as they appear in others but especially as they are directly experienced, even by normal people. To be able to recognize anything for what it is, we must first be able to identify it. We must know something about its characteristics. A person unfamiliar with the jungles of Africa may be in the presence of danger without awareness of it, simply because he does not know the sounds or the visible signs that to the native mean the presence of danger. The experienced mariner can forecast many things about the coming weather because he knows the meaning of changes in the sea, the winds, the sky, etc., which mean little or nothing to a novice. So the average person, in his ignorance of the kind of changes in behavior, in thinking and in feeling that occur in mental disorder, may experience these changes without realizing what is happening to himself, or observe them in other persons without realizing their meaning.

This book is for the layman. Therefore, nearly all technical terms have been omitted. A long word has never been used where a short one would suffice. Illustrations have replaced definitions, and stories, as it were, of life among schizophrenics have replaced the usual kind of text. Most of the cases were obtained firsthand from studies of the individuals in a hospital setting. A few were carefully selected from the literature of psychology and psychiatry. Each of the cases illustrates some facet of what it feels like to be mentally ill.

1. Florrie and

the accusing voices

Florrie has been selected for our first study because her case is unusually easy to understand, while it also makes clear how mental disorder can develop.

Florrie is a slender blonde woman of twenty-eight. Her manner is very friendly, and she is quite normally intelligent. She is neatly dressed and well groomed. She is rather striking because of her very large grey-blue eyes, the musical quality of her voice and her grace of movement. There is something else striking about her, too. She is schizophrenic.

There is nothing about her manner or conversation, however, which would suggest to anyone that she is a "mental case." You could talk to her for half an hour or more on many topics without noticing anything unusual, unless you detected a small degree of nervous tension, a touch of anxiety or a note of depression. That she could possibly be "insane" would certainly seem incredible. As to present concerns, she would probably seem a bit preoccupied about her difficulty in holding jobs. She might also tell you that she has been living with her father since the death of her mother, or confess that she has been worried about her sweetheart, because she is unsure of his feeling toward her.

Florrie was born in Sweden, and was brought to this country when she was twelve years old; her family settled in Wisconsin. She speaks excellent English, although with a slight accent. She studied hard in high school, made a good record, and went to work after graduation as a typist and receptionist for a firm of lawyers. At the age of twenty-two, she was hospitalized for several months with tuberculosis, but recovered fully.

Florrie was working in an office when some distressing experiences occurred. She got the impression that unfavorable comments were being made about her. Among conversations going on near her at the office where she worked, Florrie heard repeatedly, or thought she heard, such expressions as "no good," or "she's no good." Again, she felt that she heard someone remark, "She was raped." Florrie thought that this might refer, somehow, to her. Once, while walking down a street, it seemed to her that a woman's voice remarked, rather loudly, "She's immoral." Florrie was shocked, felt painfully self-conscious and much disturbed.

There were other remarks which seemed to refer to her boyfriend's feelings toward her. For example, someone said, "He doesn't like her," and once she heard the comment, "He really despises her." Florrie was not always sure that the people who made these overheard comments were talking about her, or had her in mind, but at times she felt strongly enough that they *were* about her so as to be greatly disturbed. She noticed that such remarks were never made in face-to-face contacts with people, that is, never directly. She states: "They tricked me that way. The talk was always when my back was turned." It was often in a low tone, "awfully soft talk," sometimes a whisper, or somewhere between a whisper and ordinary speech.

Another kind of "talk" seemed also to refer to her sweetheart, but this was unfavorable to *him* rather than herself. For example, when someone said "Her boyfriend really isn't much," Florrie felt that this might refer to her own boyfriend, because she was quite aware of his shortcomings, and of the fact that others did not regard him very highly. She was troubled about this, she says, because she loved him despite his defects. She was also disturbed because of her fear that the unfavorable remarks about herself might have reached him and affected his regard for her.

Questions may be raised at this point whether, or why, experiences such as these should be regarded as marks of mental disturbance. If Florrie really heard the comments, and felt that they referred to her, why not dismiss the matter as no more than the kind of occasional misunderstanding to which all of us are subject at times? Who has not mistaken something overheard as referring to himself, and learned later that it did not? Surely more than this is needed to suggest that Florrie's mind was becoming disordered.

At this point we need say only that when such errors occur again and again to the same person and in a variety of situations, something beyond the ordinary is indicated. However, apart from the fact that a person with so strong an inclination to misunderstand what he hears is unusual, it is also of practical importance that he will very probably soon be regarded as a somewhat peculiar person, and that such repeated mistakes may result in a variety of social difficulties.

In Florrie's case, however, we may go a step further than this and question whether, to begin with, she really did hear all these remarks.

Some clues were provided in certain conversations, such as the following:

> PSYCHOLOGIST: Why are you scowling?
> FLORRIE: I don't think you should talk to me like that.
> PSYCHOLOGIST: Like what?
> FLORRIE: Something about not thinking much of me.
> PSYCHOLOGIST: When did you hear me say that?
> FLORRIE: Just now.
> PSYCHOLOGIST: But I said nothing at all just now.
> FLORRIE: It certainly sounded like your voice.

On another occasion the conversation took a similar turn:

> PSYCHOLOGIST: You seem anxious this morning.
> FLORRIE: Of course, I'm anxious.
> PSYCHOLOGIST: Why should you be?
> FLORRIE: I'm afraid of shock treatments.
> PSYCHOLOGIST: Has anything been said about your having shock treatments?

FLORRIE: You said, when I walked into the office: "I'm
sorry, but we've got to give you some shock."
PSYCHOLOGIST: But I said nothing of the kind.
FLORRIE: I don't see why you contradict it.

For a short period Florrie did some typing for me. She was
unsure of her ability. One morning she seemed unhappy.

FLORRIE: Maybe you should get somebody else.
PSYCHOLOGIST: What do you mean?
FLORRIE: Somebody else to do the work.
PSYCHOLOGIST: But why should I?
FLORRIE: If you're not satisfied with me.
PSYCHOLOGIST: But I *am* satisfied with you.
FLORRIE: You don't sound like it.
PSYCHOLOGIST: What did I say?
FLORRIE: Something about I'm too slow, or dumb.

It was apparent that Florrie was "hearing voices." It seemed
likely that some, and possibly most, of the "talk" she had heard
might have been of the same character.

how it began

If we assume that Florrie started out as a normal girl, what
was it that brought on the strange experience we have described?

As a child she tended to be "on the serious side." She was
sensitive, inclined to worry, and was very close to her mother.
She did well at school, was a good student. She was sociable,
and as she grew up developed several hobbies. She took violin
lessons, joined a hiking club, liked to dance. Her mother was
very strict, and Florrie and her sister were not allowed to date at
an age when other girls were doing so. The mother was especially strict on matters relating to sex. She insisted strongly on
regular churchgoing. Florrie referred to her mother as domineering; for example, she forced the girls to eat everything put on

the table. This sometimes led to arguments and made Florrie nervous. "After I grew up," she states, "she kept on treating me as if I were still a child."

On graduating from high school, Florrie worked for several years as a stenographer. She lived with her parents and appears to have been fairly well adjusted during this period. Then her mother became ill to the point of invalidism, and for over a year Florrie labored under a heavy strain of overwork in caring for her mother while holding a job. Her mother died, and this loss laid a heavy depression upon Florrie's exhaustion.

About this time she was dating a man with whom she fell in love. She expected to marry him, but he found excuses for delay. Florrie had misgivings as to his interest in her. It was during the early courtship period that she began to be troubled by comments that seemed to suggest that all was not well with her romance, that her friend did not really care for her. The character of the "talk" changed when Florrie was forced into a sex relationship by her lover. It was then that the references to rape began. The sex relationship continued on a voluntary basis, to be followed by further anxiety as the "talk" became concerned with her morals, and charges that she was "no good" were frequent.

Florrie denies that she experienced feelings of guilt over her affair, and says that this was because she was very much in love and expected to marry. She states: "I realized that people were making accusations, but I thought they could not really know anything about the affair because there was no way they could have found out. Yes, I was puzzled. I couldn't understand how they could seem to know about it."

After several months of hospitalization Florrie made a fair recovery and was discharged. She obtained a position, lived with her father, and apparently got along well enough for about six months. Then, one day, the trouble began again. She heard her name and the name of her lover mentioned by neighbors. She also heard unfavorable references to her morals. It was soon disclosed during an interview that she had resumed her former relationship with her lover.

Florrie complained also that she had at times been kept awake by "night noises." These, it developed, turned out to be the voices of her neighbors discussing her. There had been threats that the police might come for her, that she must move away from the neighborhood, or that she would be returned to the hospital. In anguish she had cried out that she would give up her lover. Some of these experiences had a rather nightmarish quality.

So much for the behavior that led Florrie to "need a psychiatrist." The surface meaning of her illness, at least, must already be apparent, since the connection between the symptoms (the "voices") and her love affair is clear enough. Florrie had, as many would say, a guilt complex about her sexual conduct, and this complex must have had something to do with the talk she heard, since it was full of charges of wrongdoing.

It was noted that Florrie was sensitive as a child, and one who took things seriously. She was raised with strictness and authority, and it is therefore safe to surmise that she took her mother's teachings much to heart with respect to morals.

Another important feature of Florrie's personality was her tendency to forcibly banish thoughts that were unpleasant. She once acknowledged in an interview that she was "good at it," that is, at pushing anything out of her mind that was distressing. Florrie's face assumed, in fact, a characteristic expression at such times. It became a bit tense, stiff and resolute, as if she were almost literally closing her mind against an uncongenial thought.

The first "talk" she heard concerned her boyfriend. He was not, it seems, a person she felt proud of; despite his attraction for her, she was aware that he was little admired by others. Doubtless, many girls would find such considerations rather painful. We can also be fairly sure, from what we know of Florrie's mental habits, that she succeeded in banishing such thoughts from her mind. Then began the sexual phase of the affair, which would immediately create a painful conflict for a girl with Florrie's upbringing. Here again, Florrie reacted with her usual tendency to repress thoughts which were intolerable. She felt very little guilt

[handwritten marginal notes:] Unconsciously pushed out of mind   repressed thoughts always come back sometimes in other forms

about the affair, she told me, giving as the reason that she expected marriage.

the voice of conscience

What really happened to Florrie's conscience that she felt no guilt over what, in the light of her standards, was certainly sinful behavior? Before attempting an answer to this question, certain experiences of quite normal people may be cited. Suppose that a small boy has just done something strongly forbidden; for example, that he has masturbated. Now he ventures among others, very conscious of what he has just done, and also very conscious of it as something he has been told is shameful in the eyes of everyone. Perhaps he hears his name spoken (or what might sound like his name), or picks up such words as "we saw it," or "what he did," or some such phrases (or what might resemble such phrases). At once, his thoughts centered upon himself, he concludes that he has been observed, his act discovered, and that he is the subject of scandalous and humiliating comments. It seems to him that he *hears his guilt voiced by those about him.*

Again, many have banished an unpleasant thought, only to find it intruding from time to time, as if trying to get back. Suppose a person has done something he is not very proud of (to keep to the same kind of example) and has tried to force the matter from his daily activities, but is aware every so often that the *"voice of guilt" is still speaking to him* from somewhere in the background of his mind. Conscience, as we know, is often referred to as a voice, or as expressing itself as a voice.

Now, to get back to Florrie, our account so far suggests that what happened was that she had banished her "sex conscience," but that it continued to speak to her in a new way, in the guise of a voice from the outside world. It came in to her as if from someone other than herself. It appears that Florrie's trouble is really a kind of conscience disorder, as if this part of her mind were split off, or operating outside its normal channels. Finally, it is rather striking that the voices were sometimes heard as a whispering, since conscience is often said to whisper its reproofs, warnings, etc.

If we are now to truly understand the meaning of Florrie's trouble, the next question to ask is why this all happened. Why did her conscience break away from the rest of her personality? Why didn't it stay with her, as other peoples' do, and simply cause her the usual and normal kind of guilt-suffering so long as she continued with her questionable sex behavior? If we are to understand mental illness, not as a meaningless breakdown of the mind's machinery, but as something that makes sense in terms of normal human feelings and needs, then we must know why Florrie's conscience came to act upon her as a "hallucination" instead of in the usual role of guide and critic.

The answer hinges on the reaction to guilt feeling. There are, doubtless, people to whom guilt means no great distress so long as it is hidden from others. It is less painful for them to contain the shame within than to face the judging voices of society. But there are some, like Florrie, for whom this is not true. For her the condemning judgments (which she did not accept) were easier to face than her own self-reproaches. It was easier to *feel* free of guilt, herself, despite the disapproving comments. It was easier, in other words, to be merely *called* "no good," than to *believe* it.

Florrie suffered less emotional distress, therefore, from the charges she "overheard" than had she been directly attacked by her conscience. She thus escaped from herself, though at the price of a serious mental disturbance. Such an outcome can make sense only if the escape was worth what it cost.

From this a fact of great importance about mental illness becomes clear: that this behavior, so puzzling outwardly, and often so apparently pointless, has a purpose in relation to the emotional life. In some way and in some degree it serves a need, does some immediate good, even though from a larger point of view it may cripple or badly handicap a person in other ways.

For Florrie it reduced the pain of guilt at the cost of producing troubling "voices" and finally hospitalization.

Something further is needed to explain why Florrie reacted as she did to the experience of sex guilt, since we may safely suppose that many girls have done what Florrie did without developing an emotional disorder as a consequence. We have noted that Florrie had a strong conscience in this region of behavior and that her guilt would therefore be unusually distressing. Beyond this, however, it seems that the various parts of Florrie's mental make-up were somewhat less tightly knit together than they might have been, which is just a way of saying, in view of what happened, that a kind of separation or "splitting off" occurred in part of her personality, with the result that she experienced no conscious guilt when normally she would have done so. Every mental hospital contains people of whom it might be said that the mind has become separated into two parts, one of which talks to the other.

Finally, Florrie's illness developed at a time when she was laboring under a considerable degree of fatigue, and many would stress this factor's heavy contribution to her illness.

the machinery of hallucinations

Sometimes a case turns up in which the close linkage between conscience and "voices" is seen with unusual clarity. A young missionary with very high morals was at work among primitive people. He was troubled by erotic thoughts because of the scanty clothing of the native women. He tried to subdue these thoughts, but the sexual tension increased. Finally, he lost control, and "in a frenzy" attacked one of the women. A mental breakdown followed immediately, during which he heard "voices" charging him with immorality. Under treatment aimed at helping him to become less rigid in his high standards, and more tolerant of his weakness, the "voices" from outside subsided, and the accusations now seemed to have their source within his own mind, sometimes as a "soft whisper." Conscience, in other words, was coming closer, and was approaching its more normal location and form. His guilt was no longer coming to him through voices, but was being faced directly. When the mental "whispers" ceased, his conscience bothered him about his deed quite normally, but when conscience became too intense, the whispers took its place, and repeated to him what his conscience had been saying. Such an experience shows the true origin of the voices heard by the mentally ill, at least in this type of case.

As to the actual mental machinery of the hallucinations, a simplified version of the way in which it comes about will suffice at this point.

Most of us can, of course, quite normally "hear" our own thoughts simply because thoughts are so often expressed in the form of words, as a kind of inner speech. This may be observed easily when we silently "talk to ourselves." This kind of experience is more vivid for some people than for others, but patients have been reported whose thoughts, expressed in inner speech, are so vivid that they actually fear that others too may "hear" them (especially, perhaps, when they feel guilty about the character of their thoughts).

Ordinarily, words which have the sound of actual speech come to us from other people. We have, therefore, a *strong habit* of perceiving words which have this speech quality as coming from others. When, in nervous illness, thought-words become so vivid—because of strong guilt feelings, for example—as to approach the quality of speech, they may accordingly be heard as coming from another person. (An example of this is occasionally provided when a patient says he is puzzled at hearing what seem to be his own thoughts spoken by others.) Finally, the words heard are no longer recognized as a part of the self.

The meaning of Florrie's strange experience may now be summed up for what it tells us about mental illness. First, there was a severe *conflict*. There had been a struggle, and at times the painful tension of indecision must have filled her mind.

The core of the disturbance in her mental life was evidently in the region of social behavior. The conflict involved her relationship to other people and her knowledge of what society disapproves. Her symptom—the voices—represented the judgments of others upon her, their accusations and censure. It was in the social sphere that Florrie repeatedly showed disturbances while in the hospital. She believed that other patients were talking about her, and she twisted the meaning of what she heard. Yet Florrie made a quite normal score on intelligence tests and on other tests of mental functioning and alertness, and she performed well enough at work assigned her at the hospital.

Another feature of Florrie's disorder was that she did not understand what had happened to her. That is, she did not realize that she was ill, that the machinery of her conscience had broken under stress and was working in an unusual and remarkably roundabout way. She accepted what she heard as real, and was convinced that people were actually talking about her. The only exceptions to this were a few occasions when she hallucinated my voice and was later able to accept my assurances that I had not spoken the words she had heard. Of course the *realness* of such experiences in mental illness is one of the factors which makes treatment difficult.

Again, the act of repressing painfully conflicting thoughts appears importantly related to the disturbance. Florrie tried to escape the conflict between her sex behavior and her morals by forcing from her mind the realization of the "wickedness" of her indulgence. Her statement that she did not feel guilty showed that she had succeeded in this (helped along by expectation of marriage). The case suggests a connection between *forcing something out of mind* and the occurrence of new events which seem to take place in the environment. It looks, in other words, as if what a person represses may return or reappear to him in a different form.

As our account shows, and as other cases will fully illustrate, the symptoms of illness may have other sources than guilt feelings about sex behavior. The first signs of Florrie's disturbance

were overheard remarks which seemed to belittle her lover. The
first conflict centered about the painful consciousness that the
person she loved was not respected by others. At a later stage of
her illness the picture was again altered, as seen in her account
of experiences in which she heard threats, while at home, that she
would be returned to the hospital. Here the "voices" were related
to her own anxiety.

Finally, Florrie's case illustrates that the symptoms of mental disorder may be seen as the solution of an emotional problem. Distressing as were the accusations she heard, they were,
for Florrie, a lesser evil. Being called names she felt were unjust
was easier than living face to face with her guilt.

2. Marcella:

the social outcast

Like many other illnesses, schizophrenia exhibits a variety of forms. The differences from one case to another are often more striking than the similarities. Marcella is also a schizophrenic, but her symptoms differ in important features from those of Florrie.

Marcella is small, dark in coloring, inclined to be plump. She is always neatly dressed, has pleasing features, a courteous manner, and speaks softly. She is twenty-nine, married, has three children. The family is middle-class; Marcella's husband is an accountant, moderately successful. The children are of school age, and the oldest boy is twelve.

Her story begins in a way which soon becomes very familiar to students of mental disorder. Marcella "couldn't get along with people." More particularly, she had trouble with her neighbors. Her present neighborhood is, in fact, the third in which distressing things have happened, and the third from which she has pressed her husband to move away, and for the same reason.

The following is an illustrative conversation:

PSYCHOLOGIST: What sort of trouble did you have with your neighbors?

MARCELLA: Well, they did a lot of things to bother me.

PSYCHOLOGIST: What kind of things?

MARCELLA: Some little things, and some pretty serious things.

PSYCHOLOGIST: Can you give me some examples?

MARCELLA: Well, what bothered me a lot was their getting into the house when we were away.

PSYCHOLOGIST: Could you be sure of this?

MARCELLA: I certainly could. Things were damaged. Sometimes they took things.

PSYCHOLOGIST: How much damage was done?

MARCELLA: Well, not a lot, but they had no right to enter the house.

PSYCHOLOGIST: What sort of damage was done?

MARCELLA: Well, once a chair was scratched. There was some colored stuff spilled on a rug. Once they tore a window shade.

PSYCHOLOGIST: Anything else?

MARCELLA: Sometimes things were missing. I never found them.

PSYCHOLOGIST: Things get lost in every home.

MARCELLA: They weren't lost. They were taken.

PSYCHOLOGIST: Did they do anything else?

MARCELLA: Sometimes things were moved. They changed things around.

PSYCHOLOGIST: Why was this done?

MARCELLA: Just to bother me. To show they had been in the house.

PSYCHOLOGIST: You mean, that was the only reason it was done?

MARCELLA: The reason was to annoy me so much that we'd move out of the neighborhood. It was all to get rid of us.

PSYCHOLOGIST: What do they have against you?

MARCELLA: I don't know.

PSYCHOLOGIST: Is your whole family unpopular?

MARCELLA: Well, my husband gets along all right.

PSYCHOLOGIST: Is it the children?

MARCELLA: I don't think so.

PSYCHOLOGIST: Then it's you they want to get rid of?

MARCELLA: Yes, it's me.

PSYCHOLOGIST: And you have no idea why?

MARCELLA: No.

Marcella is a nervous person who is at times much distressed by excessive noises. Often big trucks pass in front of the home, not only rumbling heavily, but making the house shake in a way very trying to her nerves. She became increasingly irritated, and in exasperation concluded that these truck movements were, like the other annoyances, part of the design to force her to move away. The noise and the vibrations took on a *personal meaning*. They ceased to be part of the world's work, going on independently of her existence. They became *intentionally* irritating, that is, malicious. Marcella telephoned the police to complain, and when no action was taken she phoned several trucking companies to repeat her angry protests.

for impersonal actions; took personal offense to things that were not directed to her.

Marcella is, in fact, no stranger to the local police. She has appealed to them on a number of occasions for protection. From time to time she has made her accusations directly, and has become rather notorious for the verbal floggings she has given her neighbors and the angry disputes in which she has been involved. Although in her calm periods she seems seclusive and even rather shy, she can be emphatically aggressive when aroused. She complains also that the neighbors have listened in on her telephone conversations, and expresses the suspicion that there may be microphones about, installed during her absence as a means of recording her conversations. She explains, "I thought it was partly just for annoyance, and partly to pick up things they wanted to use against me when they got a chance."

feelings of persecution (complex)

paranoid

While there were moments when Marcella was willing to consider the possibility that she might be mistaken in some of the incidents she reported, she was strongly inclined, for the most part, to place the blame with her neighbors.

PSYCHOLOGIST: You say you have no idea why these people treat you as you say they do?

MARCELLA: No. I've wondered about it a lot.

PSYCHOLOGIST: You've tried to get to the bottom of it?

MARCELLA: Yes. I've even read books on mental illness.

PSYCHOLOGIST: What did you learn?

MARCELLA: Well, I didn't find the answer.

PSYCHOLOGIST: Do you mean you thought you might be mentally ill?

MARCELLA: Well, no. I thought I might learn what would make these people act so strangely.

PSYCHOLOGIST: You mean you think your neighbors may be mentally affected?

MARCELLA: I've had that idea.

PSYCHOLOGIST: That it is they, rather than yourself?

MARCELLA: Yes. I thought once of seeing a psychiatrist.

PSYCHOLOGIST: Why?

MARCELLA: To see if he could explain why they act the way they do.

PSYCHOLOGIST: Would you ask him about yourself, too?

MARCELLA: Maybe I would.

PSYCHOLOGIST: What would you ask?

MARCELLA: Well, whether there's something about me that makes people treat me this way.

PSYCHOLOGIST: You wouldn't ask him whether he thought they really do mistreat you?

MARCELLA: No.

PSYCHOLOGIST: Why not?

MARCELLA: Because I'm sure they do.

how to recognize a "paranoid"

Probably many would recognize Marcella as illustrating what is commonly referred to as a persecution complex, meaning that she falsely interprets the behavior of others as being unfriendly, hostile or threatening. At this point, note that her illness may be seen as having, on the surface, two main features. First, she believes that she is disliked, and that there is a movement to force her, by a variety of abuses and annoyances, to leave her neighborhood. Her inclination to believe this, and the false interpretations which result, *are* her "mental illness." Second, she reacts to this treatment with strong resentment and retaliates with angry charges and with attempted legal actions.

To say that Marcella falsely interprets the behavior of others as unfriendly naturally raises the question how we can be sure of this. Isn't it possible that, for some reason not yet brought out, Marcella *was* much disliked by her neighbors, who *did* take various measures to express their feelings toward her and to exert pressure with the hope of forcing her to move away? A case was reported from a psychiatric hospital in which a young man was judged as suffering from delusions of persecution because he complained that certain people seemed to be observing his daily movements about the city in the course of his work. He felt convinced that he was being followed. It turned out that he had actually been under observation for several weeks by investigators employed by his wife, who had become suspicious of his fidelity.

Such a case is exceptional, however, and there are ways of being sure that such interpretations as Marcella made of the actions of others are truly the symptoms of mental disorder rather than an actual case of community action against an undesirable person.

First, we note the fact of *repetition*. Marcella, at the time of our description of her behavior, had been living in the third neighborhood in which such ideas had developed. Her earlier experiences had been very similar. There were the same incidents, irritations and petty annoyances, all viewed, not as accidental, but as intended to make her aware of the hostility of her neighbors and to force her to move away. Even during her hospitalization the familiar pattern was repeated. Marcella became quite anxious one day after hearing a reference to "certain cases to be discussed by the medical staff." This caused her to conclude at once that she was to be transferred to another hospital. Into this innocent comment she read a personal meaning. As usual, this meaning was in terms of rejection. Her habit of feeling herself unwelcome was working even within a mental hospital!

Our question whether Marcella is truly delusional may be restated. Has she for unknown reasons actually been subjected to persecutions, year after year and from place to place, or has she more likely a psychological quirk of some kind, that causes her again and again to believe herself unwanted wherever she goes?

If, from a study of Marcella's personality, we can find evidence that such a quirk exists, and discover how it has developed, we will have added support for the view that she has repeatedly mistaken the behavior of the people about her. Another *of delusions* way of confirming this may be found in the *lack of plausibility* of some of Marcella's ideas. Would it be likely, for example, that her neighbors, solely to annoy her, would break into the house in her absence to move a piece of furniture, or to leave a stain upon one of her rugs, or to carry away an article of small value? Or would it be likely that truckers, supposedly in cooperation, would intentionally make undue noise in passing her home? In many cases of this kind it is possible to infer from the improbability of the patient's story that we are dealing with a disorder of thinking rather than with an authentic report of facts.

Very often this matter of plausibility hinges on *motives*. In talking to such people as Marcella, and listening to the account of their treatment by others, the first sign we may meet which raises a question about mental health may be that what they say about others does not correspond well with what we would regard as the way human beings normally behave. The story told by one patient, for example, of the persecutions he had suffered in revenge for a rather minor offense might seem not at all unlikely until he tells us that this offense occurred eleven years earlier! When we find that he accepts without question the persistence of vengeful feeling for so long a period (and involving pursuit by the "enemy," not only from city to city, but from state to state) there are grounds, it would seem, for doubting his interpretations of events. It may be surmised that his judgments as to how far people will go for revenge are seriously faulty; his knowledge of motives is poor.

We conclude then, that Marcella's experiences represent a mistaken way of interpreting or "reading" peoples' actions. Such mistaken readings are her mental illness. An attempt may now be made to explain, by way of her personality and her background, how such a tendency can develop.

growth of a "complex"

A key to Marcella's illness is clearly seen in some of the things we discover about her girlhood. She was reared in a home in which there was much discord between the parents. It was not a home in which a child would learn to feel secure. Her father and mother were too busy with their troubles as husband and wife to give much thought to their role as parents. Neither Marcella nor her sister ever felt close to either parent. About her mother she said: "I never tried to talk my problems over with her because she never seemed to try to understand. She would brush me off."

Of her father Marcella recalls certain impressions vividly. When he returned home from work he rarely greeted her. He might even pass her on the street without speaking. She recalls several small incidents, such as the night when, returning from work, he found her sitting on the staircase and stepped over her without a word. She thinks his apparent lack of love, or even of interest, was occasioned in part by distaste for her appearance. She was inclined to be fat, and thinks she was unattractive otherwise. Her father often criticized her walk, and jeered at her plumpness. Marcella said that although these comments were sometimes made in a joking tone, "they hurt, nevertheless." He once said to her: "You'll have a tough time finding a husband."

Marcella had a girlfriend of whom she was very fond. One summer this friend became acquainted with some new people whom she regarded as "aristocratic," and wished to cultivate. She gave a party and carefully selected her guests in order to impress the new friends. Marcella was not invited. Later her girlfriend realized her snobbishness and apologized, but Marcella felt crushed. "I cried several nights. It took me a long time to get over that."

She dates, from a variety of such experiences of girlhood, the beginnings of a feeling which continued to grow—the feeling of being unwanted.

elaborates her feelings of rejectedness

Marcella says she was a fair student at school, but that socially she tended to keep to herself. She belonged to no groups, attended few social functions, had very few dates. She was very conscious of being overweight, and at home was often reminded of this by her parents. She was conscious, too, of feeling at a disadvantage in the matter of dress. Her parents could not afford many new dresses, and Marcella thinks this was one reason she did not go out as much as she might have. Another reason was that she often felt painfully ill at ease. This was especially true at dances. She was rarely asked to dance, and recalls some very uncomfortable ordeals in the role of wallflower. Such experiences strengthened her feeling of being unwanted or of being unacceptable.

Regarding her courtship, Marcella says she believes her husband was in love with her, but that "I don't think he was exactly proud of me. He rarely took me out anywhere. He had friends who were dating but we never dated with them." Marcella felt that, while she might be attractive to her husband, he preferred not to exhibit her. "He just didn't want to show me around." This, again, did not raise her confidence. Her husband's mother lived with them for a while, also his brother. Marcella felt that these people did not like her, and this resulted in some friction between her and her husband. Her marriage was nevertheless, fairly happy until the time when her symptoms began to appear.

She was devoted to her children, but sensitive to anything which might be viewed as a slight to them. Since they were, in a sense, part of her, she extended her own feelings upon them, and tended to fear that they might be treated as she had been.

It is clear enough that out of the influence of a certain kind of father and mother, of certain defects in physical appearance, and of a variety of experiences sharply etched in her memory in which people failed to respond favorably to her, a *habitual* feeling of rejection became a very active and sensitive part of Marcella's personality.

the "complex" is a habit

It is important to emphasize at this point that *ways of feeling*, like ways of moving, of speaking and of thinking, may become habits. Like other habits, moreover, habits of feeling may become very strong. Marcella's habit of feeling unwanted was so strong that it caused her to misread what was going on about her. Like a fearful person who sees threats and dangers everywhere, or like a guilty person who sees the pointing fingers of accusation from every direction, Marcella felt herself disapproved, belittled or slighted in a variety of social situations.

Another way of describing what happened to Marcella is to say that she continued to *react in an old way to new situations*. Her original feelings of rejection were well fitted to her father's treatment. These feelings were no longer fitted to the way people were *now* treating her. In her emotional reactions to people she was still living in the past.

Some of the ways in which her "habit" was active were quite trivial. Sometimes, in entering a building, for example, or in taking her place in a waiting line, it might happen that at the moment of her arrival several other people suddenly appeared and moved in ahead of her. Marcella wonders if such happenings are entirely accidental. They make her feel brushed aside. She finds such incidents offensive, almost as if people are deliberately taunting her, or even as if, as she once put it, "Life itself is trying to tell me I'm less important than others."

Again, in approaching a counter in a large store, she noted that very often the clerk would appear to find business elsewhere as soon as he saw her coming. At times this makes her feel that she is somehow known to the clerk as her neighbors know her, that is, as an undesirable person. At other times she may feel only that there is something about her that simply does not appeal to people. She has also noticed small incidents while her children were at play which suggested that they too are slighted, scorned or treated with less regard than others are.

[handwritten margin note: (Gordon Allport' functional autonomy) creating an attitude at a particular moment in childhood. Attitude develops. May now do the same things but not for the same motives. Attitude does not relate to the past anymore]

The feature of *repetition,* seen in the fact that her feeling of rejection became active in several different neighborhoods, is just what we would expect, of course, if this feeling had become habitual. Even in a hospital setting, as mentioned, the habit continued to function. We could therefore hardly agree with Marcella that the solution to her problem lies in moving out of her community and seeking a new one. Wherever she goes, the habit will go with her.

scorn made her furious

Up to this point we have dealt with only one side of Marcella's emotional problem, namely, that she misunderstood her neighbors. Had this been the whole story she would probably have been regarded simply as a rather seclusive person who made few friends and rarely had a caller. She was known, on the contrary, as a sullen and hostile person who on occasion attacked those she regarded as annoyers with furious outbursts of indignation. She could be, in short, a highly aggressive individual and as such, a community problem.

What did this hostility mean? The answer lies, in part, in what is commonly called temperament or "emotional nature." Another person in Marcella's place might have reacted in a quite different way. The kind of social hurts she suffered might have led to a very compliant sort of personality, with striving to avoid rejection by being very anxious to please and by giving in to others in every way. Or it might have led to an "aloof" personality, as an attempt to keep away from others emotionally, to avoid being hurt. Again, it might have led to efforts to excel others and thus to force recognition and acceptance.

Marcella was different. While she might occasionally withdraw or pretend indifference when she felt snubbed, she more often retaliated. Slights made her angry. When people hurt her she wanted to hurt back. The record contains numerous instances of her attacks, usually sharply verbal, on those whose actions she felt were offensive. Marcella was not, in short, a person to take affronts "lying down." She was a fighter.

Some features of her behavior which would otherwise be somewhat puzzling become understandable by way of this chronic bitter resentment. The exceedingly trivial grounds on which she occasionally denounced her neighbors (for example, a misplaced household article, a knotted clothesline, some mud on her doorstep, a scratch on her furniture) are strongly suggestive of a person whose exaggerated touchiness is, in reality, the finding of excuses for venting vengeful feelings. She was like a person who, full of unrelieved resentment, is looking for trouble or seeking an excuse to discharge dammed-up feeling. This resentment strengthened her tendency to find offenses and annoyances everywhere.

Marcella herself was not aware of the part her resentment played. She believed the offenses to be real without seeing that her feelings were a source of her belief. There was no evidence that she knew what she was doing, that is, that she was *consciously* using small excuses to strike against those she felt had rejected her. In this, she illustrates, of course, a very common feature of human behavior, namely, that we are not always aware, or fully aware, of the nature of the feelings or motives behind our actions.

What can we learn about mental illness from Marcella's behavior? First of all, that repetition of certain kinds of experience in early life may leave not only a lasting but a dominating influence upon the adult personality. The total effect of this upon Marcella had spoiled her feeling toward people for many years, had involved her family in numerous disturbances and several times forced her hospitalization. It had also made her very unhappy.

We learn, again, that resentment can become so intense as to amount to an emotional disorder. Probably all of us are familiar with the impulse to retaliate that comes when one feels he has been belittled, or in some way treated with disrespect. This urge to retaliate tended to overwhelm Marcella. She knew her outbursts were ill-mannered, and she was unhappy about her neighborhood reputation, but when affronts—or what she thought to be affronts—occurred, her anger surged up, and the impulse toward bitter attack upon the offending person was too strong to restrain. In this, of course, her behavior does not differ greatly from that of any person, who, in certain situations, finds his emotions difficult to check.

The most striking feature of Marcella's disorder was the *false meaning* she gave to the small events of everyday life. A gate left open was the result, not of carelessness, but of the malicious action of her neighbors, perhaps designed to let in dogs who might damage her garden. A jagged hole in a rainspout could not have come from weathering; it showed, rather, the vandalism of those who hoped to force her to leave the community through this and countless other abuses. To an extreme degree, Marcella took things personally.

to justify feelings of persecution

what about the queer ideas?

To sum up, we may say that the essence of Marcella's illness was that she wrongly believed herself disliked, that because of this she was angered, and that both feelings together caused her to see herself as victimized in a variety of ways. Can we say that this is truly the whole story? A further question might well be: Her rejection, her hostility and her habit of taking things personally are understandable, but what about her farfetched notions of what people were doing to her? What can be said of her belief that passing drivers were annoying her by intention; that neighbors would risk entering her home in her absence to inflict minor damage solely to annoy her, or that they would make excessive noises, like slamming doors, for the same reason? Is there not something peculiar about such ideas?

The question could be made even more pointed if we include examples from other cases similar to that of Marcella. Thus, one patient complained that motorists, all day long, raced their motors as they drove past her home, in order to irritate her. Another thought that passing planes were sent to observe her movements as she walked about the hospital grounds.

Since having "queer" ideas is, of course, very close to what people commonly regard as the chief feature of mental disorder, this aspect of Marcella's behavior is of unquestioned importance. Some of our discussion of it will be postponed to a later place. It may be noted here, at least, that Marcella's *knowledge of people's motives* appears to be rather poor in quality. If this were not true she would, we would say, "know better" than to think that her neighbors would resort to such unlikely and roundabout maneuvers as those she reported. For all her strong feelings, and admitting that feelings can strongly influence our perceptions, it would appear that Marcella must lack to an important degree a knowledge of people that would enable her to dismiss such notions as extremely improbable, "on the face of it."

Knowledge of people of this kind is of course what everyone normally acquires in the course of everyday life. It means learning how strongly people ordinarily feel about certain things, and how much effort they are likely to put forth in order to achieve certain goals. It means learning, for example, not only what sort of things usually anger people, but how angry they are likely to become over a particular provocation, and how long, ordinarily, such anger may last.

Returning for a moment to our earlier example of the patient who believed himself still threatened because of an eleven-year-old offense, we note that he had evicted from an apartment some men he regarded as dangerous characters, for failure to pay their rent. He believed that they maintained surveillance over him from one job to another, and even from one city to another. Since he believed them to be probable members of the underworld, he felt that their vengefulness might extend as far as taking his life. Whatever the emotional factors which led to the formation of such a belief, the question is raised whether it could have persisted with adequate knowledge of human motives.

We cannot take for granted that all human beings are alike in ability to accurately read and comprehend the feelings and motives of others, any more than we can assume they are alike in intelligence, talents, etc. Like everything else we must learn, ability of this kind depends importantly on opportunity to acquire it. The fact that we so often find, in the background of personalities like Marcella, a marked tendency toward social shyness, a failure to mix well, gives a hint as to one source of defects in this ability. It seems inevitable that, through failure to live close enough psychologically to others, some people should grow up with a lack of the kind of knowledge of others, acquired through everyday experiences with them, which would help to check the growth of false perceptions.

Marcella and Florrie became ill in very different ways. Both felt rejected, but for different reasons. In each case what appeared as disturbing behavior on the part of others was found to be a kind of outward reflection of a deep-seated emotional conflict within. In each, the influence of experiences with a parent was clearly of great importance.

The next member of our introductory group will present, again, a widely different picture in details, but will further illustrate the way in which internal stresses may strangely alter the familiar world of everyday events.

3. Marilyn:

lady in dilemma

Marilyn is twenty-eight, small and rather slender. Her eyes and hair are black. One does not at first notice how pretty she is, because of her heavy shell-rimmed glasses. Her clothing is that of a person of moderate means, but in excellent taste. Her intelligence is much above average, and there is a quality of sensitivity and refinement about her.

She was born in Georgia. She has just enough "colored blood" to be recognizable as part Negro, although she says she has often "passed" as white.

She was one of nine children. Owing to the early death of her father, her youth was spent in a painfully struggling and badly underprivileged family. The mother, by extraordinary labors, maintained good discipline in raising her family, sent them regularly to church, and strongly stressed good morals. She inspired them to study hard, with the result that all but two finished high school and two others managed to get through college.

At eighteen, Marilyn married a boyhood sweetheart and went to New Orleans to live. The marriage was a happy one except that she wanted a child, and none came. After two years her husband was killed in an industrial accident and she returned to her home. Marilyn remarried, but has been separated from her husband for several years. He is a fairly successful lawyer. There were no children, and Marilyn has moved about considerably since the separation, working from job to job, and sometimes from city to city. It is easy for her to get jobs, as she is a very efficient medical technician.

You could talk to Marilyn, as to Florrie, for some time without noting unusual behavior. She is amiable and responsive, her answers to questions are mostly logical, and her thoughts are well connected.

Marilyn's case was one of several in the writer's experience, closely similar, which illustrated with unusual clarity the fact that in mental illness what appears to be a pattern of events in the behavior of other people may be in reality an outward reflection of a disturbance in the patient's own emotional life. There were in fact some extraordinary parallels, incident by incident, between Marilyn's case and certain others.

She was brought to the hospital because she had been very depressed, and because like Florrie she had been repeatedly troubled by comments made by others which she felt had personal meaning for her. Sometimes, she said, when people nearby were speaking to each other, it seemed to her that what they said was either about her or was somehow intended for her to hear. She began to notice these strange comments after her decision to leave her husband. She became very restless, left the Southern city where she and her husband had lived (and which will be called Southtown) and traveled about the country, staying for short periods in different cities.

An important part of Marilyn's story may be taken from the records of her interviews at the hospital.

> PSYCHOLOGIST: Who said these things you heard?
> MARILYN: Different people.
> PSYCHOLOGIST: Did you know them?
> MARILYN: Some I did, some I didn't.
> PSYCHOLOGIST: Did you understand what they meant?
> MARILYN: Sometimes I thought I did. Sometimes I was puzzled.
> PSYCHOLOGIST: What did you think they meant?
> MARILYN: Sometimes it seemed that they meant I should go back to Allan. But I never will. Not after what I went through.

PSYCHOLOGIST: Did people you didn't know say things like this?

MARILYN: Sometimes. It was pretty queer. Why should anybody want me to go back to him?

PSYCHOLOGIST: What were some of the things you remember hearing?

MARILYN: Well, there was a landlady once where I was staying. I told her I was separated and going to get a divorce. Later she said, "You'll never get a divorce." It sounded strange, the way she said it. Didn't seem to fit what we had been talking about. Besides, how could she know?

PSYCHOLOGIST: How did you feel about this?

MARILYN: It worried me. It seemed as if these people knew something about me. It seemed as if there was a kind of movement to get me to go back to Allan. I was afraid they would force me to do it. If I'd have known who it was, maybe I wouldn't have been frightened. But I didn't know who it could be. That made it harder.

PSYCHOLOGIST: Was all the "talk" you heard about going back to your husband?

MARILYN: No, that was queer, too. Sometimes what people said seemed to be like a warning. Like somebody might say, "Don't go back to Southtown," and maybe I hadn't even mentioned it, or said anything about wanting to go back.

PSYCHOLOGIST: In other words, what some people said suggested you'd have to go back, and what others said suggested that you should *not* go back.

MARILYN: That's right. They were different kinds of people, too.

PSYCHOLOGIST: How do you mean, "different"?

MARILYN: Just not the same kind of people, at all.

PSYCHOLOGIST: What kinds of people were they?

MARILYN: Well, the things that really nice people said, like decent, religious people, were all to make me stay away from Southtown, where Allan is. They seemed to mean: "Don't go back to him."

PSYCHOLOGIST: What were the other kind of people like?

MARILYN: Well, just the opposite kind.

PSYCHOLOGIST: Like what?

MARILYN: Just lower-class people. Ne'er-do-wells. Street trash and foreigners.

PSYCHOLOGIST: What sort of things did they say, or seem to be saying?

MARILYN: I can't remember what they said.

PSYCHOLOGIST: Well, just what sort of things?

MARILYN: Things that meant I'd have to go back to Allan. Things to drag me down. To degrade me.

PSYCHOLOGIST: Degrade you in what way?

MARILYN: I don't know.

PSYCHOLOGIST: In what way do you think it might be?

MARILYN: I'm not sure. Maybe my morals.

PSYCHOLOGIST: You mean, degrade you sexually?

MARILYN: That seemed to be the general idea.

PSYCHOLOGIST: What do you think all this means?

MARILYN: I don't know. I don't know what they're up to, or how they can know so much about my affairs. There must be something behind all this.

After several months of hospitalization Marilyn's mood was less depressed, and she talked less of "influences" and "forces." She was discharged, and began fairly soon to travel about with the same restlessness she had previously shown. She sometimes left a position because of the disturbing "talk," which made her nervous and affected her work. Finally, after some months of wandering, she returned voluntarily to the hospital, which was near Southtown.

It was at once noted that Marilyn was a bit confused as to why she had returned. She wanted a "statement," she said, of her status as a discharged patient. She did not, however, seem to be clear about what she had in mind, or what purpose the "statement" was to serve. She did not, in fact, appear to be greatly concerned about it. She discussed it in a perfunctory manner, and readily left the topic for other matters. It was apparent that there was another reason for her return, whether she was aware of it or not.

At this point the following features of Marilyn's experience may be noted:

She hears, or believes she hears, comments relating to herself and to her marriage, made by people unknown or little known to her. *Conscious speaking?*

The comments suggest that "forces" are at work about her. There seem to be two such forces, one opposed to the other. They are in some way competing to influence her behavior. One would drive her toward, the other away from the city near the hospital where her husband resides.

One force is good, the other bad. One is associated with socially acceptable or "virtuous" people, the other with "the lower-class trash."

Is it possible to make sense out of these strange events? Recalling what was learned from the study of Marcella and of Florrie, a beginning may be made with the surmise that what appeared to Marilyn as puzzling events about her, was in reality the *outward reflection of something active within her.* This idea that the experiences of the mentally ill are very often a seeming change of the external world of people and things, brought about by what is actually an inner disturbance of the emotional life, is basic in understanding these disorders. The phenomenon is called "projection."

In its simplest form it may be seen in many familiar incidents in which a sensitivity of some kind affects perceptions. A boy with his first long trousers, for example, is mentally *set* to notice signs in others that his appearance is attracting attention. The smile of a passerby (perhaps over an amusing story he has heard), the slight frown of another (perhaps over a perplexing thought about the day's work), are at once taken to be critical reactions to the new attire. The boy thus unknowingly *creates*, as he goes along, a whole series of such reactions. Being highly conscious of himself, he assumes that others, too, must be conscious of him. *—from feelings within the individual*

Among the reports of Marilyn during the early period of her illness, it was noted that she often became upset at mention of her estranged husband. During interviews at the hospital she repeatedly referred to him in highly unfavorable terms. There were times when she denounced her husband's long record of abuses, of brutality, selfishness and infidelity. She left no grounds for doubting that her sole feeling toward him was revulsion and resentment approaching hatred.

But on other occasions the matter was not so clear. In discussing her motive for returning to Southtown she was asked if she felt there might be some reason beyond those she had given. She replied with the question: "You mean some kind of sentiment for somebody?" This thought was entirely her own. Once asked whether she would ever, under any circumstances, consider resuming her marriage, she answered, after a period of silence, that she could tolerate it only "if he would stay in one part of the house and I would stay in the other." Finally, when asked if she would be willing to talk to her husband if he could be persuaded to come to the hospital, Marilyn broke into tears for the first time and said, "Yes, but I would probably go to pieces."

From this and other evidence it was clear that Marilyn was in the throes of an intense emotional struggle, which at times came very close to the surface. The usual question must now be asked: Why, of the countless instances in which a broken marriage has left the parties concerned with mixed feelings, should the conflict in this case have resulted in mental breakdown?

To begin with, the conflict was intense because the emotions were strong. A fixation of remarkable power bound Marilyn to her husband. She was a person of deep feeling, who could say: "Heaven or hell couldn't turn me against a man if I were really in love with him." Marriage was for her a sacred bond. In emotional make-up she was the opposite of those shallow people who move lightly and casually from one "love" relationship into another with little disturbance beyond surface eddies of feeling. She was one of those who fall hard and recover slowly. Love for her husband was anchored in roots which had not broken despite many stresses.

These stresses had been severe. Coarse-grained and callous, Marilyn's husband had added contempt to abuse. Further sharpening the conflict was a marked difference in culture. Her hus-

band drank, was profane and uncouth, while Marilyn was refined
in sensibilities. Her conception of marriage was romantic and
idealized, while that of her husband was crudely sensual. Her
natural inclinations were toward self-betterment; she wanted
to cultivate "nice people." Her husband's tendency was downward; he was not fastidious, and sought amusement where he
could find it.

A few somewhat veiled remarks hinted of conflict in the sexual region. Her husband's erotic nature was abnormal, Marilyn
thought. He was "animal," accused her of not being "low-down"
enough to suit him. She was revolted, her standards of decency
and dignity were violated. Since there was evidence, however,
that she was herself rather strongly sexed, it is possible that she
may have discovered impulses within herself, through her husband's "degraded" inclinations, which led to a repugnant clash
with her self-esteem and personal standards. She was proud,
highly moral and religious. Incompatibility in the sexual area
may have added much to the more basic sources of conflict.

To sum up, the findings suggested that what Marilyn could
not face, or could not acknowledge, was her profound and en-
slaving emotional bondage to a man who stood for a way of living against which her whole spirit revolted, whose humiliating
treatment had shaken her morale, and who had aroused in her a
revulsion from herself through erotic temptations she could not
accept. All of her pride and her standards demanded that she
reject her husband, yet a need and a desire of extraordinary
strength made her powerless to do so.

Somewhere during the period when this conflict was at its
height, the beginnings of disorder made their appearance. What
Marilyn had to have was a way of changing the personal meaning
of the compelling urge to return to Southtown (and her husband) once she had managed to move elsewhere. When her emotional hunger and restlessness threatened to come to the surface,
its true meaning had to be altered or disguised. Unable to admit that the "force" she later complained of was her own need,
she sought to shift the blame, like the child who seeks to escape

the charge of unacceptable behavior with the protest: "They made me do it." The essence of Marilyn's delusion might have been expressed as: "I don't want to go back to him, but 'they' are trying to force me to it."

Exactly where and when this tendency first became active would not be easy to determine. Some accidental incident or impression probably provided the germ. It is when, as we know, our needs and anxieties are most acute that we tend to grasp at straws. It is then that we seize upon any small support for building a comforting hope. In Marilyn's case it may have been an encounter with the "bits of talk" that so often turn up in the history of such cases.

She told of a casual conversation with a fellow passenger on a plane trip to New York. The passenger remarked, in telling an anecdote of someone she knew: "She isn't going to get very far with it." Marilyn said: "It seemed to me there was something queer about the way she said it. It didn't seem to fit the conversation." She felt that the remark was somehow related to her own attempt to get away from her husband, and that the "she" referred to was herself. She was puzzled, she said, that this unknown person should seem to know something of her affairs. Nonetheless, she took the remark to suggest that her attempt to break away would fail, and this because "someone" would block her effort.

It was from scattered and seemingly trivial experiences such as this that Marilyn built her belief that there was a "movement" under way to force a return to her marriage. Once this belief was established, her problem was, in a sense, solved, meaning that she was relieved of having to own up to a desire she felt was deeply humiliating.

It was earlier noted that Marilyn's disordered behavior was connected with two different social settings. The forces which seemed to be striving to influence her were expressed now in the actions of "nice" people, and again in those of "low" people; the latter impelling her toward her husband, and the former away from him.

Anyone who, in the throes of the acute phase of a love attachment, has experienced the remarkable effects of almost anything linked by association with the person concerned, can understand what happened to Marilyn in encounters with the kind
of people ("degraded characters") who reminded her of her husband. Though they stood for the traits that had aroused her revulsion for him, they tended to arouse, also, the emotion that had
kept the conflict alive. Because she could not acknowledge this
emotion, the effect of this stirring-up, "in the depths," came to
consciousness muffled and distorted, as it were, in the form of
the strange "comments" which seemed to threaten her with a
return to further degradation. By the same logic, "nice, decent
people," were symbols, too, being associated with that side of
her personality that had revolted against her marriage.

Marilyn's tendency to avoid emotional distress by removing
the personal meaning from certain experiences was illustrated
in other ways. Because of her deep attachment, for example, the
reality of her husband's cruelty and apparent lack of love for her
was too painful to bear. He could not, she wanted to believe, be
truly responsible for what she had suffered at his hands. He must
be under the influence of malign, external forces. She felt that
his behavior could not be explained by her treatment of him.
There must have been something else that made him act as
he did, something bigger, that was too much for him. This being
true, she could not really resent the things he had done.

Marilyn's belief in strange forces whose intention was somehow centered upon her may be seen as in part the product of a
tendency which was present before her disorder developed. She
was inclined toward fatalism, was interested in astrology, believed in "destiny." She told of experiences that led her to believe
that people in general are helpless against fate. Certain family
misfortunes had convinced her that unhappiness was to be her
lot.

What can be learned about mental illness from the study of
Marilyn's case?

It may begin, it appears, with a clash or struggle of opposed feelings. Love and hate for the same person were here at war. Such conflicts of feeling are of high importance among the experiences that lead to disorder. To be torn by attraction and repulsion is for some people an intensely distressing ordeal which puts a great strain on whatever enables the mind to stay in one piece. Another and perhaps more frequent kind of conflict—to be illustrated in other cases—is that between a strong feeling of dependency, toward a parent, for example, and an equally strong urge toward independence and initiative.

From the literature of mental illness we may take a case similar in that a strong attachment was opposed by other feelings, but illustrating a different way in which the problem was solved, though by the same basic "delusion method."

A young man of excellent education and scholarly background found himself irresistibly attracted to a housemaid "of little education or personal charm." This attraction, which he could not comprehend, was in sharp conflict with his self-esteem. He had been trained by his father to "take great pride in developing reason and strength of character." The attraction "not only contradicted his most unshakable principles, but violated his conception of himself as strong-willed and superior." At a loss to understand the girl's attraction and influence, he first theorized that she might be using hypnosis upon him, or that she had drugged his food. As her power over him continued to grow, he finally concluded that the girl was no ordinary mortal, that he was being victimized by a supernatural force. She was, he decided, a "goddess in disguise . . . who was irresistible by virtue of her origin. . . . This solution enabled the patient to preserve the fiction of his own strength of character . . . since he had been vanquished only by a supernatural power." [1]

Here, again, the way out of a conflict was found in the belief in a compelling external force, in order to avoid admitting an emotional need. This will again be seen in Chapter 6 with special clearness in a case made famous by Freud.

A final feature of Marilyn's disorder may be marked as fairly characteristic of mental illness. She was sincerely deceived by her strange experiences. She was not *aware* that a disorder had begun to affect her mental processes. Just as a person may unknowingly suffer from a physical malady—in the early stages, at least—so Marilyn, although much puzzled when people she hardly knew seemed familiar with her affairs, never questioned the genuineness of these happenings. It did not occur to her that the occasional seemingly queer behavior of persons about her could mean that the normal workings of her mind had become impaired. It appeared to her only that *people* were behaving strangely, rather than that her own perceptions were becoming disordered.

An illustration of this was seen in the case of Marcella, who thought of consulting a psychiatrist to learn why her *neighbors* were saying and doing certain unaccountable things. Hospital doctors are quite familiar with the patients who protest that it is a husband, or a wife, or some other family member, who should be hospitalized, rather than themselves.

Why is it that persons becoming disordered do not perceive these changes within themselves, just as, for example, a motorist may perceive that his car's performance is becoming impaired?

One reason why people are often not conscious of the onset of mental illness is that the emotional state during which the disorder begins may not be favorable to self-observation. A person in the midst of emotional distress is commonly too absorbed in it for much self-analysis. Anxiety does not favor observing one's self in this way. A person in conflict may be too unhappy to think clearly; he is too preoccupied with the problems he faces. Add to this, too, that there are marked differences, from person to person, in the inclination and the ability to make such observations. Many are so immersed in the feelings of each moment that they rarely or never seem to "stand aside" from experience to take a larger view.

4. on the ward

A visitor passing through the wards of a state mental hospital once made the comment that, while no two patients really looked alike, there was nevertheless a certain sameness about them.

The impression of sameness is easily understood and comes from the total effect of a visual survey of hundreds of human beings, most of whom are sitting inactive, with faces reflecting, mask-like, their inner vacancy, abstraction or preoccupation.

Yet, that no two are really alike, even on the surface, is the more important fact, for it may be seen as a token of the *individuality* of each case. The likeness of expression, or the lack of it, is in part a marking of the vacancy and sameness of hospital life. It is in the differences that we will find much of the meaning of mental illness. For each of these people is a "personality."

the impostors

Ronald is a rather sad looking youth of twenty-six years. His skin is pale, his eyes are light blue; his hair is a thick shock, seldom well combed, of many strands. His features are delicately molded, and he might pass as attractive but for his somewhat washed out expression. When he smiles, his face lights up in a way that would warm you, but he rarely smiles.

If you were to ask Ronald about his family he might tell you that his mother and father visit him every week. At least, he might add, they were supposed to be his mother and father. Such a strange remark would doubtless lead to further questions, and then Ronald would tell you that the people who come are not really his parents, but merely look and act somewhat like them. As to how this can be, Ronald speaks a bit vaguely about plastic surgery. He is vague, too, about the reason for such an impersonation. He is unable to tell why anyone should attempt such a masquerade.

Such doubting of the identity of closely related or well known persons is not uncommon in the mentally ill. It is not, of course, the sole mark of disturbance in Ronald, but has been selected as an illustration. What can be the meaning of so strange a disorder in the recognition of people?

Ronald was an "overprotected" child. His mother was devoted, guarded him carefully, and was inclined to advise him in everything he did. As he grew older there were occasional sharp frictions when her protectiveness tended to limit his growing need for freedom. He was treated, he felt, like a child. His privileges were fewer than those of his friends of comparable age. Because of this he felt humiliated. He was called a "mama's boy," and resentfully complained that he "could not do things like the other fellows." Ronald's father was stern, strict and punitive. At times he would be indulgent, and probably, in his way, loved his son, but he appeared to feel that he must at all times be authoritative. He constantly warned, admonished, oppressed with his questions. "It was like a 'third degree' sometimes," said Ronald. "He'd question me about my schoolwork or about what I did when I was out with the fellows. Sometimes he made me feel like a criminal."

Ronald grew up a dependent, immature boy, tending to cling to his parents, suffering painfully under his father's brutal discipline, occasionally rebelling in intense anger against it, yet becoming deeply disturbed when, after a flare-up, he felt rejected. "I was miserable when I was 'in the doghouse,'" Ronald tells us. "I felt frightened and sort of lost."

The meaning of Ronald's strange ideas about his parents, during his illness, may be understood in terms of his mixed feelings toward them. He loved them very much. His eyes often teared when he spoke of them. Toward the masqueraders who visited him he felt cold, distant, mildly hostile. Toward these people he felt, it seems, as he often felt about his parents before he became ill. The "substitutes" provided an outlet for his hostility. To furnish this outlet seemed, in fact, to be the *purpose* of the delusion. To love *and* hate the same person or to suffer at the hands of those we love, is for some an exceedingly painful experience.

To Ronald's disordered mind his parents had "doubled" into two sets in order to relieve him of the tormenting conflict. His "true" father and mother he still loved, and *could* love, now, without any of the emotional pain of the hurts they had inflicted. For these hurts, and the resentment they aroused, could now be attributed to other people, who were somehow not his parents. *Ronald's delusion was a way of denying that his loved ones could be cruel to him.*

In the same ward with Ronald is a long-faced, rather apathetic man named Max. He is twenty-nine, but one feels an impulse to refer to him as a "boy," for like Ronald he is immature and dependent. A few days after his arrival at the hospital Max exhibited an interesting variation of the "masquerader symptom." He thought that several other patients and two or three of the ward attendants were "putting on an act" for his benefit. Certain remarks and gestures suggested to Max that they were not really what they appeared to be, but were "agents" in a sense, who had been "planted" at the hospital. Their presence, moreover, had an important personal meaning for Max. "They've got something to do with my being here," he said. "I watch them, and sometimes I get a sign, like some kind of advice." These "agents," it appeared, were operating for his special benefit. They were on his side, and their purpose was to protect and instruct him.

This curious notion was but one of several marks of disorder in Max's behavior, but it became less strange as more was learned about him. For long periods, although finished with schooling and over twenty-one, he had been unemployed. He spent the days at home with his parents, claiming he was unable to get work. Max was in fair physical condition, and was not exactly lazy, but showed some anxiety about getting a job. He seemed to need little variety, and was fond of staying around the house. He was very close to his father, was, in fact, a kind of "father's boy" who continued, though approaching thirty, to take a good deal for granted with regard to paternal help and guidance.

Hospitalization was frightening to Max. It took him away from the secure parental haven and thrust him among strangers and into a "cold" environment, far from all things known and familiar. Many patients find the move from home to hospital something of a shock. For a person like Max it brought on a spell of panic.

In this emergency the delusional tendency that Max exhibited in other ways now came to his rescue. To meet his need and to stave off the terror, the impersonal attendants became, in his perceptions, transformed into guides and protectors (we might say, into "father substitutes"), and the indifferent patients into friendly "agents."

Max's delusion of identity was, to be sure, a symptom of illness, but it was a symptom with a purpose. It was a false belief, but the *reassurance it gave was real*. After a few days, when his new surroundings became more familiar and less threatening, the delusion vanished.

Karen, a tall, gaunt woman in her early forties, is another patient who shows occasional confusion in identifying people. At times she reports events, as an eyewitness, so improbable (or impossible) that it is evident that she has had visual experiences of an abnormal kind. As Karen describes them, these experiences are highly suggestive of the kind of dreams that a normal person might have, but there is no doubt that for her they are very real.

Karen became doubtful of my identity, because she was convinced that I had a "double." She was therefore not always sure which of the two persons she was addressing. She was led to this conclusion in a way which was really quite logical. In one of her very vivid "waking-dream" experiences (technically called an "hallucination") the writer appeared to her engaged in actions which she found impossible to reconcile with his character as she had come to know it during many interviews. However, since she accepted the reality of these experiences, she felt forced to conclude that there must be, therefore, not one person but two.

These examples of uncertain or false identity illustrate that what appears on the surface to be the same symptom, may arise in quite different ways. In two instances, it is notable that the symptom either solved a conflict or reduced an anxiety.

the virtuous one

On the women's ward Florence sits apart from the others. Sometimes for an entire day she speaks to no one and may not answer if spoken to. She is blonde, Polish, in her middle forties, and a widow.

Florence resisted questioning when admitted to the hospital. This was especially true when an attempt was made to explore her emotional life during the beginnings of her illness. She talks freely and heatedly, as if she were compelled to talk, and she is hard to interrupt.

She is sure that certain people are trying to force her into immorality. They are using hospitalization as a means of putting pressure on her for this purpose. "If anybody thinks that if they keep me here they can make a certain something out of me, they'll find out how wrong they are." (What do you mean, a "certain something"?) "I mean a prostitute. If I'd have been willing to do that they'd probably have let me go home from Receiving Hospital. . . . Not for millions would I do anything like that. . . . Not for millions would I do anything bad."

In a case described earlier (that of Marilyn) the idea was introduced that a desire, when painful to acknowledge, may become transformed so that it is felt as a pressure or influence "from the outside." This has been expressed in the formula: "It is not I who wish it, but *they* who are forcing me to do it." We may find here the clue to the accusations repeatedly made by Florence and to the pressure she appeared to be laboring under. Her insistence on her high morality, in the absence of any charges made, suggest that she was troubled by an inner conflict. One is reminded of a braggart whose boasting becomes loud enough to arouse a suspicion of secret cowardice, or of the queen in *Hamlet* who protested her virtue so strongly as to prompt the often-quoted comment, "Methinks the lady doth protest too much."

In a conversation during which there had been no hint of question concerning her morals, Florence made such remarks as: "If anybody thinks I'm so nervous because I haven't got a husband anymore they're wrong. . . . I've been living alone for two years and I've never had a wrong thought on my mind." Again and again she stressed the theme of her purity in the face of temptation: "If I went out with all the men who want me I'd be the biggest prostitute in the world." She cited evidence of her attractiveness, and proclaimed that it would be easy for her to remarry if she wished, but that she did not want to.

From Florence's history we learn that her upbringing was very strict, and that she was inclined to be over-conscientious in her early years. In her reference to sex, the repeated phrase "low and filthy" gives us a clue to her attitude toward it. We surmise here a conflict between sharp and rigid moral standards, and the normal needs of a healthy, sexually abstinent woman. Florence could not admit these needs. By charging others with the intention of forcing her into sexual license, she escaped the pain of having to confess what were to her shameful desires.

the poisoned heart

Harold is a thin, sandy-haired man of about 40, who looks older because of his deeply lined face and heavy beard. Like most patients in a mental hospital, he usually sits in the same chair day after day. Harold will do small tasks around the ward fairly willingly, but complains of a feeling of weakness if heavy work or a regular routine is suggested.

Several years ago Harold suffered an attack of food poison-ing. He explains that while he made a partial recovery from this, some of the poison remained in his system, with the result that too much exertion causes his heart to "labor." At such times it be-haves, he says, "like an auto motor with too much load."

Physicians have assured Harold that his heart is quite sound, and that the effects of food poisoning are not what he believes them to be, but he is little affected by such advice. He persists in consulting doctors, and appears to be sincere in his conviction that his heart has been organically damaged. Among the ef-fects of this, he says, is "a loss of ability to carry out normal pur-suits. For years it has kept me from getting ahead." Harold has a wife and one child. On a recent visit to the hospital his wife an-nounced that she planned to obtain a divorce. Harold appeared to be a little shaken by the news.

His family requested his admission to the hospital when it was realized that his fixed ideas about his health were irrational. He had been unemployed for over a year, after quitting several jobs because he felt too weak to work. During interviews at the time of his admission to the hospital, Harold talked readily and with much detail of the history of his ill health since he was poisoned by food, and of the blighting effect of this great misfortune upon his career, his family life and his personal hap-piness.

Some of his statements concerning the working of the body included rather strange ideas, which he persisted in defending when questions were raised regarding their accuracy. He seemed little interested in improving his knowledge of physiology, how-ever, and clung rigidly to his conviction that all his physical com-plaints—of which he had several—were traceable to the same source.

For many people there would, of course, be little mystery about Harold's case. "The man is simply lazy," they would say. "He doesn't want to work, and is using a fake illness as an alibi."

On the surface this explanation might seem plausible, but there are some things it does not account for. Harold's family, while impatient and unsympathetic about his supposed illness, admitted that when employed he worked too hard at his jobs, and that as a youth he had taken his responsibilities over-seriously. He had, moreover, spent money he could not afford on doctors.

During mental examinations he twice broke into tears, unaccountably. There were times when he talked rapidly and in great detail about the different jobs he had held, talking as if he felt compelled to do so, and could not stop. He also showed a marked preoccupation with seemingly unimportant aspects of a variety of topics, as if there were matters he wished to avoid discussing (as people sometimes do when they are anxious to skirt around an uncomfortable subject).

The story of Harold's delusion of ill health begins in his teenage years. He was a good student in high school, conscientious, and with ambitions to become an engineer. When family finances forced him to abandon plans to go to college, and to take instead a rather menial job in an engineering company, Harold was deeply disappointed. He worked for eight years with the engineering company but made little progress.

Some phases of the work interested him, but others seemed sterile and tiresome. He felt that he was not appreciated, nor much respected. His morale was shaken when he enrolled for two night-school courses in engineering subjects and found them not only dull but difficult. "I began to realize how much there was to engineering," Harold said, ". . . it's a pretty hard thing to admit . . . you realize your inadequacies. Those courses knocked my confidence out. I was surprised how quick I lost my confidence."

He became increasingly unhappy with his work, and resentful that his family's need made it impossible for him to give it up in order to seek something else. He recalls: "I didn't seem to be getting anywhere. There were times when I'd get disgusted and want to quit. I saw others get promotions but nothing came my way. I knew there would be a blow-up in the family if I quit. I got extremely anxious. Most of my pay went to the family. I was working very hard and putting in overtime. People have accused me of not holding jobs. *I had as much trouble quitting jobs as getting them.* My pay was the backbone of the family."

It was during the period of this conflict and anxiety that Harold suffered food poisoning. On his recovery he returned to his engineering job, but his output of work declined and he was released. From this point on his work record became irregular; ill health became increasingly chronic. He had unexplained accidents on the jobs, and he was often late for work. Finally he ceased to look for employment.

Harold's illness provided the solution to an otherwise insoluble problem. It led to release from uncongenial work, and it also took the edge from his sense of personal failure. Thus, he states: "I had the brains and ability to go farther, but my illness has kept me back." Again: "If I hadn't been forced by necessity to take jobs below my ability I could have had jobs that paid a lot more than I ever made."

Such confident statements may be doubted, however, in the light of certain evidence that Harold's morale had been seriously impaired early in his career. He said: "I felt very bad when I had to quit school and take that routine job. I was really shaken. I think I began to feel inferior then. I remember I got headaches and had nightmares." Harold's "illness" may be seen in the setting of a decline of morale as well as pressure of family needs.

Was Harold mentally ill? There was no reason to doubt that he was as truly delusional concerning his physical ailments as was Ronald about the identity of his parents, or Marcella about her persecutions. It would not, of course, have been necessary for Harold to have truly believed in his "poisoned heart" in order to have excused his job failures in the eyes of his family. No more than a sham was needed to cover his "secret" from the judgments of *others*. But to spare *himself* from the admission of personal failure he needed a sincere belief in physical weakness.

Harold had "lost his nerve," but it was easier for him to believe that he had lost his health. He may be compared with the man who, having failed to gain a promotion through lack of ability, convinced himself that he had been victimized by favoritism and "office politics." He may be compared, in fact, with any person who manages to find a way of thinking which removes or relieves the pain of humiliation.

anger as an illness

Willie is a slender, dark-haired boy who has been hospitalized for three years. He is twenty-eight, but appears much younger owing to his cherubic face, light beard and clear skin. He does not look like a college graduate in engineering, either, but he was working at his profession at the time he became emotionally ill.

There is nothing "cherubic," however, about Willie's personality. A hospital aide once referred to Willie as "sinister," but this was doubtless a reflection of the aide's uneasiness when Willie was around. There is, nevertheless, something distinctive about Willie, and this something is a deep, restrained, but all-pervading hostility. He looks taut, or brittle. His face is cold and fixed, but with the tension of one trying to hold together a mask of poise, yet very close, much of the time, to having it burst into pieces. With never a sign of open rage, or even a hint of candid and healthy anger, Willie is quietly and steadily "mad at the world."

He is really quite subtle about it. At the time of his admission to the hospital he was described as "courteous without warmth, a sharp-cornered personality; has a kind of acid quality about him." When spoken to, there is often a calculated delay before he responds, as if to indicate that he acts at his own initiative, not that of others, and will reply when he feels ready. He frequently refuses to return greetings, this with a stiff, impersonal air of abstraction, as if he did not hear. He is skillfully evasive in parrying questions and keeping the questioner at a distance.

When invited to join a group of patients for discussion with a staff member, Willie came, but sat apart from the rest. His indifference was aggressive, ostentatious. He would bring a newspaper, which he would either rattle, or pretend to read. He would ask the time, with a glance at the exit door. On the rare occasions when he participated in the discussion he seemed to strive for cynicism or for paradox. Without apology he might introduce a radical change of subject.

Willie does not have delusions, nor does he "hear voices." He expresses no "queer" ideas, and his speech is intelligible most of the time. When it is difficult to understand what he says, it is because his thoughts are so colored and distorted by his mood. He is not really trying to communicate, but only to vent his bitterness. Compared with the people earlier described, Willie doesn't have any *symptoms* of mental disorder. Yet it might be said, just as certainly, that his entire personality is ill. His behavior is so thoroughly penetrated with hostility as to affect all of his social relationships. While, as mentioned, Willie is not delusional in the usual sense, he says many things which are not true, or in which a small truth is much exaggerated, and he appears to mean what he says.

Here we touch closely upon the experiences of normal emotional life. Anyone who, under the influence of resentment or indignation, has said things he does not fully mean, has had a sample of what is needed to help in understanding the state Willie is in. We may, of course, really mean such things *at the time* we say them, but realize later how much our feelings were responsible.

Yet such a mood, when it becomes chronic, continuously twisting out of reason much or most of the course of mental life, may result in a true emotional sickness. When a mood of resentment or hostility is intense enough, and lasts long enough, and affects a large enough portion of a person's behavior, he may be considered mentally disordered, just as a person whose feelings of depression are profound and long lasting is regarded as disordered.

To understand how Willie got this way we must, as usual,

retrace certain features of his emotional history. As a child he was inclined to be shy and unaggressive, the type often pushed around by others. He was very obedient, and sensitive to punishment. His parents, while very protective, gave him little affection. They believed in discipline by punishment, and this punishment was at times merciless. Punishment was by rejection as well as by scolding. The parents were demanding, and punishment was frequent. The mother was the dominating one, whom Willie admired and feared. Her treatment fostered a dependency and an anxiety which caused Willie, many years later, to feel immature. He remembers how much he wanted acceptance by his parents, and the hurts that came when he failed to receive it. He recalls the efforts he made to gain attention and affection. Beyond question Willie had known what young children often experience when "banished" by parents. It is the feeling of "being *lost*," and it is catastrophic.

Willie's mother and father saw that all his physical needs were satisfied, but they left him emotionally and spiritually starved. Years later, in his better moods, when Willie was asked whether he thought his parents really loved him, he replied, "I suppose they must have. They bought me clothes."

The effects of this emotional conflict of childhood showed clearly as Willie moved further, with maturity, into the larger world beyond the home. Habitually he felt unsure of himself; unsure, that is, of his acceptance, unsure that others would, on acquaintance, like and respect him. At school he feared failure beyond the ordinary because it had become so closely linked in his mind with the agonizing thought of being abandoned.

In response to this habitual insecurity there grew up, over the years and gradually, an increasing resentment. Willie still remembers the occasional surges of angry feeling that came when he failed to receive the attention he craved. Later there were spells of irritability and argumentativeness, and even a few of rage, in which he became threatening. At other times he became depressed. He once left home, went out into the suburbs, cut himself superficially with a razor blade in an assumed attempt at suicide, then phoned his parents to come and get him. Such behavior is, of course, easily recognizable as that of a person who, feeling unloved or outcast, attempts in a desperate way to awaken sympathy or arouse concern. Willie became increasingly tense and seclusive, and lost a job because of inattention and wool-gathering. Because of his rages, his threats and his self-injury, his parents consulted a psychiatrist, and Willie soon found himself in a mental hospital.

While there was plenty of evidence of feelings of inadequacy, depression and, in general, "unwantedness" in the background of Willie's emotional life, it is equally clear that, as in the case of Marcella, resentment and hostility came to dominate the picture. It was clear, too, that Willie's continuing emotional dependency upon his parents was the source of his bitterness, for his bitterness came from rejection, which stung him as it did because of his need, never outgrown, of a close bond with his parents. A direct glimpse of the source of this dependency was occasionally seen when his parents visited him at the hospital. It was then noted that they spoke to him as to a very small or very young boy, that there was much quizzing, admonishing and critical comment, and that following these visits Willie's cold rage was more than usually evident.

All, or most of us, know how it feels to sulk after hurt feelings. Willie had been painfully and repeatedly hurt, and his sulk had become continuous. All of us, again, have allowed an emotion aroused by one person to affect our treatment of others. Willie's bitter mood, rooted in childhood resentments, finally overflowed its original channels to spread out in every direction, and to include the whole world, to some degree, in its compass. His behavior shows that an emotional state which in mild degree is normal, becomes an illness when a certain intensity and duration is reached. Willie had much too much of what a great many of us have in smaller amounts.

design for living

A main theme of this book is that various quite normal needs and emotional states are the sources of the symptoms of mental illness. Once in a while a patient shows so clearly what it is that gives rise to strange ways of thinking as to amount, almost, to a demonstration.

Martha is a "privileged" patient, free to go anywhere she wishes on the hospital grounds. She is a tiny, rather slender, reddish-haired woman of thirty-one. She is well formed and well dressed and her features are good, though her eyes protrude slightly and are a bit distorted by the glasses she wears. She is college-educated, fluent, friendly and likable. Before her illness she was employed as a receptionist in a suite of medical offices. She is unmarried, and until recently has been living with a sister.

During early interviews, following her admission to the hospital, Martha was much preoccupied with a romantic attraction to a man she had encountered several months previously. She met this man, she tells us, in the course of her work, and became convinced that he was amorously interested in her, although her account of his actual behavior leaves ground for doubting this. She "has a feeling" that he has plans which include her in an important way; this may mean marriage, though she is not sure.

At times she feels that even her hospitalization may be, somehow, part of his plan for her, and that she is to be "prepared" for some purpose of his. He once sent her a card while on a business trip. He described some beautiful scenery, and said that he hoped that she "might see it some day." Martha thought that this was significant because "since he didn't say exactly where it (the scenery) was, it must mean he would be with me when I saw it." She managed to find hopeful meanings in other remarks he had made to her.

There were other times, however, when Martha was occupied less with her "lover," and more with her sexual needs. She took my statement that I wished to help her with her emotional problems to mean that I would, if necessary, provide her with sexual satisfaction, "since this is certainly my emotional problem." Martha was hard to convince when she did not *want* to believe something; she pounded on the desk, repeating the question, "But are you *sure* you don't mean it that way?"

The outstanding feature of Martha's thinking during the period of study, however, was her belief that there was a "plan" which, as a kind of design for her personal destiny, in a sense guided her and lay behind many of the things that happened to her. The idea of "being led" occurred frequently in Martha's preoccupations. Sometimes the things people said, or what she overheard, seemed to contain directives for her. Sometimes, also, these things made her feel that her emotional problems were somehow known to others.

"For example, there's this girlfriend of mine. I met her sweetheart. It was at her home. He was very attractive and I envied her. When he looked at me he seemed to be appraising me, a kind of penetrating look. Later on he played the piano. There was a piece of music with the words 'good little girl' or something like that in it. I felt he was sort of jeering at my aloofness from men and my virtuous life. I thought that he must have seen something about me—that I had a sex problem—that I was frustrated. Nearly every song he played made me feel that he picked it for a definite reason, that he must know something about me or about my past.

"Then there were things I called 'markers.' They were in a newspaper, or something on a billboard I passed in a bus. It would seem to hit me just right. It would fit my problem to a 'T' and I'd feel it was fate or the scheme of my life. There was a headline about some prisoners making a daring break out of jail. It hit me just like I was being told: 'If you had more courage you could break out of your inhibitions and be free to have a better life.' Everything, or so many things, seemed to mean something."

Martha's case illustrates a number of important features of the abnormal workings of the mind. Most clearly of all, perhaps, it shows the influence of *need* upon believing. In its simplest form this very common human tendency is called "wishful thinking." Martha read between the lines of her experiences, meanings fitted not to realities but her own desires. This strong tendency was indicated in her habit of saying "I have a *feeling* that (something) is so," symbolizing the influence of her emotional life upon her convictions. For example: "I've had this feeling for a long time, that he (her 'lover') knows what I need, and is working things out for me." Sometimes the tendency was quite nakedly exposed in her own words, as when Martha asked me whether I would visit her after her discharge from the hospital. When I replied in the negative, Martha said she refused to believe that I meant it. I then remarked: "Either you are delusional in thinking that I might come, or else I am being untruthful in saying that I will not come." Martha replied, "I'd rather believe that you are untruthful, and I *do* believe that you are."

Martha was inclined to see the "plan" in the background of a great many things that happened to her. Even small events, she thought, might be part of the pattern. Another way she expressed it was that, as noted earlier, "so many things seem to *mean* something." Behind what, to others, would be accidental happenings, she saw a purpose. This purpose was sometimes a realization of her hopes, like the message on the postcard. Sometimes the purpose seemed to be instructive, as in the case of the newspaper headline. Again, it might be critical, as in the words of music. Finally, it could be a sign intended to reflect some feature of her own life. Thus, when she saw a bird flying against the wind and moving backward instead of forward, it seemed like a message to convey that, despite her efforts, she was losing ground in the struggle toward her goals.

The "plan delusion" is often seen in mental patients. It exhibits a variety of forms. A visitor is seen through a window, walking toward the main office building; he is seen as an agent of the patient's family; his mission is to serve a purpose (often vague) in the patient's future. A new staff member is appointed; he has been sent to fulfill his part in a scheme which will somehow benefit the patient's interests. The writer's name is

heard for the first time by a new patient, and is perceived at once
to mean the person who will finally "grant" his release. A change
in some feature of hospital affairs is announced, and the patient sees himself as somehow the reason for this change; its aim
is to advance his interest in some way. The effect of this thought
tendency is, obviously, to *personalize* events. Beyond this, and
more important, it fits events into a larger design, and of this design the patient's needs and hopes are the center.

What does such a tendency mean? In Martha's case its meaning was clear in certain findings about her personality and background of experiences.

In Martha's family the mother was the dominant figure, who
was highly protective toward her two daughters. She was aggressive, devoted, affectionate and "caressing," but expected
much in return in the way of compliance. Her treatment of her
daughters strongly stressed the lesson that if they were to feel
secure in her affection they must give in to her wishes. In Martha,
particularly, this treatment led to a marked degree of submission. "I always felt," Martha said, "that I had to be accepted by
her, so I wanted to do everything she wanted me to. I'd feel terribly guilty whenever I'd rebel. . . . I still feel very dependent.
. . . I've never known how to cope with her. She kept me tied
to her. She did it partly by telling me there was nothing she
would not do for me if I needed it."

Among the effects of this treatment, in Martha, were certain
infantile traits which had persisted into adulthood. Another was
a failure in growth of individuality. "I've never had a personality
of my own," she observed. "I'm easily influenced. I can adjust to
anybody because I don't have much of a character. It's part of
my immaturity." Martha grew into a woman who, despite a fair
degree of adultness of surface behavior, had a deep and child-
like need of the emotional support of a strong "mother-figure."

In her early twenties she and her older sister moved into an
apartment of their own. The mother often visited, but Martha
transferred much of her dependency to her sister. The latter then
married and Martha was tempted to return to her mother, but

succeeded in resisting the impulse. There were stormy scenes as the mother attempted to regain her dominance. Finally Martha was offered an excellent position which meant removal to a distant city and fairly permanent separation from her mother. Shortly after accepting this position she began to show some of the signs of mental disorder which have been described.

The "plan" in which Martha now began to believe was the work, she surmised, of the business associate to whom she was much attracted. He had been helpful in a kindly and authoritative way. She had felt, before her illness, that he might be romantically interested in her. This feeling now became a near-conviction. Since he was an influential person, with "connections and contacts," she began to feel that much of what happened to her might be a consequence of his roundabout way of "taking care" of her. The feeling of being guided entered into much of her daily activity. Life became filled with directives. She was repeatedly struck by the *timing* of events. She felt that it could be no accident that they happened at times which gave them special meaning in terms of what her thoughts and feelings of the moment happened to be. Such things could not be accidental, she was sure.

Beyond this, her conviction that certain persons were *intended* to have important roles in her life was at times strong, though she was not always sure who these persons were. For example, she developed, as earlier mentioned, the idea that some member of the hospital staff was to provide her with "emotional relief" in a directly sexual way. Her reaction, when assured that this was not true, showed clearly the tendency of her thinking. She questioned, with considerable heat: "Well, if it isn't you, then who is it I have to find? Are you *sure* it is not you? Are you sure you aren't the one? Are you positive?"

We may sum up the meaning of Martha's disorder by saying that it illustrates, in several ways, her tendency to believe what she needed to believe. Her conviction of a design that governed the course of events was an expression of her strong need to feel that her life was *ordered and guided for her as her mother had once ordered and guided it.* Belief in a "plan" relieved anxiety and gave her comfort, just as the presence or near-presence of her mother had once done this for her. The daily evidences she saw of the workings of the "plan" were each like a word of reassurance from her mother. Her rebellion against maternal dominance had been successful, but her dependent needs continued active.

There were other examples of behavior linked with the mother's influence, some traceable to early girlhood. She often reported, during her illness, the impression that people who were strangers somehow *knew something about her*. What they said suggested that they must know something, she felt, of her past, her problems, her hopes. In discussing this, on one occasion, Martha herself suggested that it might be related to certain observations her mother was fond of making. "I remember she used to say things like: 'I know what's in your mind. I know what you've been doing. You can't keep anything from me no matter how hard you try.'"

She gave another example. "I went to visit a friend in another city. It was soon after we moved away from my mother. I stayed several nights in a hotel. I remember that each time I walked out, through the lobby, I had the strong feeling I'd be called back. I don't mean I 'heard voices.' It was just a feeling of being called. That goes back, too. Mother was always wanting to know where I was going, what I planned to do, whenever I left the house. I think it made me feel a bit guilty about it, too, whatever it was."

Again and again is found, in such experiences, evidence of the prolonged persistence, far into adult life, of habits of thinking and feeling laid down in childhood. Often, too, much of the apparent unreasonableness of the behavior labeled mental illness turns out to be, essentially, its immaturity. Some of the "abnormalities" of adults, in other words, may be behavior tendencies which, though normal to childhood, have lasted far beyond it.

Without a doubt great numbers of quite normal people have some form of belief in personal destiny which might be compared with Martha's "plan delusion." There must be many who, though perhaps rarely giving much thought to it, take for granted that there is some sort of design or "meaning" behind the things that happen to them. There may be many people, too, who would feel a kind of loneliness bordering on terror at the thought that the course of their lives depended *entirely* on their own efforts against the mercies of chance alone. Who has not sought to console himself at a moment of disappointment, for example, by saying something like: "Perhaps it is not *meant* that I should have this. Perhaps it is to turn out best, in the end, if I do not have it." We are here, of course, on the brink of issues finally related to matters of religious faith.

While, therefore, in Martha's case the tendency to find personal and comforting meanings in impersonal events was developed to an abnormal degree, its clear resemblance to a familiar tendency of normal thinking must not be overlooked.

5. the persecution complex

Very common among the mentally ill is the belief, ranging from mild suspicion to firm conviction, that other people are unfriendly or threatening. One patient may feel only that those he meets are sometimes unfavorably impressed with him, or mildly hostile. Another may think that others are definitely against him in the sense of seeking to thwart his motives and interests. Still another may fear, even to the point of terror, that the enemy is resolved to take his life, and waits only upon an opportunity.

In this chapter an attempt will be made to understand what ways of feeling and thinking lie behind this very common mark of disorder, and what kinds of life experiences prepare the way for such tendencies.

fear and delusion

In one of the cases reported by Freud, a young woman seeks legal help to protect her from the treachery of a lover.[1] He intends, she claims, to cause her to lose her position and her reputation by disclosing her "affair" with him. This he plans to do by exhibiting photographs, secretly taken, in which he and she are revealed in the act of love-making.

The patient is described as an attractive young woman, much distressed by the need of confiding her story, but overwhelmed by her anxiety. She had been living quietly with her dependent mother. Fatherless, and without brothers or sisters, she held a responsible position with success. An attachment had developed with a fellow employee, with whom marriage was impossible because of circumstances. It appears that she had been fearful of the risks of an affair, and consented only after much reassurance to visit his apartment.

In the course of their embraces she was frightened by a sound, described as a "kind of knock or tick," which seemed to come from a heavily curtained part of the room, and which her friend explained as coming from a nearby clock. Later, in leaving the rendezvous, she noticed whispering between two people who passed her on a staircase. One of them carried something box-like under a wrapper.

Immediately there arose in her mind a sinister meaning of these incidents. It occurred to her that the sound she had heard might have been that of a camera, held by a person behind the curtain, "to obtain pictorial evidence." This would explain the box-like object and the whisper on the staircase. Her suspicion at once became fixed, and her lover was unable to persuade her that her fear was groundless. Freud's observations convinced him that the lover was sincere and guiltless in the matter, and that the lady was truly deluded in her interpretation.

Some degree of anxiety in a situation of this kind is easily understood. The problem is raised by the patient's persisting suspicion in the apparent absence of any motive for such behavior in her lover, and by her failure to be moved by his protests of innocence. It would doubtless help our understanding if it were supposed that she was a person considerably more inclined to worry than most of us are, that she was rather imaginative, and perhaps that she experienced, somewhat beyond the normal degree, the fears so often linked with extramarital sex relations. It is noted that her anxiety centered in part about losing her job, and that while her mother was dependent upon her, there was apparently no one the patient herself could have turned to in case of need.

Much would have to be known, if we wished to trace such anxiety to its sources, about the personality and the experience background of a person who could find so threatening a meaning in the incident described. One can be sure only that her anxiety overwhelmed her ability to perceive reality. This, at the moment, is all we wish to illustrate. The case offers a fairly simple example for an introduction to the persecution complex of *the power of emotion to falsify the meaning of appearances.*

Next may be considered one that many might regard as nearer to "the real thing" in the way of a delusion of persecution, and that further shows the effect of anxiety upon the workings of the mind.

The patient in this instance was hospitalized because of an exaggerated and irrational fear that his life was threatened by gangsters.[2] It had all begun with a difference of opinion over a racing bet. The patient, under the influence of alcohol, had made insulting and threatening remarks to the gamblers ("bookies") who he believed had cheated him of money he had won. On sobering up, he began to worry about what he had done, and to recall what he had heard about a tie-up between horse racing and the underworld. He began to fear that he had gone too far, and that there might be a retaliation.

Soon, following the incident, he noticed strange men in the lobby of his hotel. Their attention seemed to be focused on him. They also appeared to be giving signs to each other. He became more observant, and began to feel that he was being watched and followed about. As his fear increased he secluded himself in his room; then, believing that his telephone was being tapped, he left the city on a long trip.

As he traveled, his suspicions were further confirmed. "In one city, for example, he saw a policeman examining his auto license; this meant to him that the police were in league with the gangsters and were tipping them off. Once, in a shoeshine parlor, the attendant eyed him narrowly; this was a sign that 'the grapevine system was catching up.' " [3] He provided himself with means of suicide in the event his enemies closed in upon him. His panic was increasing.

Recognized as ill by relatives, he was finally placed in a hospital. Even here his suspicions continued. He again exhibited the

belief that his telephone calls were tapped, and mistook a visiting clergyman for a gangster confederate in disguise.

The idea that fear, as a state of mind, may cause one to see
threats and dangers where they do not exist is, of course, hardly
a novelty to anyone. The story of the small boy's twilight trip
through the graveyard, and what he sees—or thinks he sees—is
familiar to all. When, however, the effects of anxiety upon behavior reach the extreme shown here, it is obvious that there is
need to know something about the personality of one whose reaction to a fairly ordinary incident could be so exaggerated.

This individual was motherless as a child; he grew up without a permanent home, without emotional security and without
close friends. There had been no one with whom he could share
experiences, or to whom he could express his feelings. At maturity his vocation tended to confirm the same mode of living. He
moved about a great deal, without permanent headquarters,
never feeling secure, never achieving a sense of belonging to the
companies for whom he worked.

These companies used "spotters" to check on the activities of
their employees. The patient therefore developed a habit of feeling under observation, and this was increased by guilt resulting
from some shady business dealings. His practice was to make
sudden changes of residence whenever he felt sure, by mulling
over what he considered adequate evidence, that he was being
watched.

It seems clear that this man's background had provided little
opportunity for close *communication* with others, and thus, for
an *understanding of the motives of others.* His vocation had
fostered suspicion and a poverty of human ties. The background
of his life thus may be said to have predisposed him quite well
for the kind of disorder he developed. He had lacked the kind
of experience and the kind of knowledge of people which would
have checked the imaginative building up of the false picture of
a gangster plot on his life.

Dr. Norman Cameron suggests that, for the persecution

complex to become firmly lodged, certain conditions must be present. Certain habits of thinking and habits of feeling favor such an outcome. Among these is the tendency to deal with human problems, not by open discussion in an effort to understand differing viewpoints, but by withdrawing, by mulling things over alone, and without making any attempts to check up on the conclusions reached. Cameron suggests that a tendency toward anxiety, and a sensitivity to certain situations, are important in the formation of this kind of behavior problem.

A fact of great importance about the people whose mental illness includes *misreadings* of the behavior of others is the frequent finding that during the beginnings of illness they were inclined to see little of friends and family members, and to spend much time alone, perhaps secluding themselves in their bedrooms. They had few contacts and little *communication* with others. These people tend not to share their thoughts and feelings. Nor do they often sample and compare the viewpoints of others with their own. They tend to be "loners" in their thinking, and so miss the many chances they might have to correct misunderstandings by learning what is going on in the minds of others.

For the same reason, delusions may grow unchecked on the wards of a mental hospital. A patient was convinced that the women on her ward were talking about her. They also made gestures which meant, she believed, that they were familiar with certain episodes of her past of which she was not at all proud. One day she was asked by an attendant to collect the names of all patients who wished to go to a dance. In the course of the "survey" she questioned many she had never talked to before, although she had been living with them for months. Soon after this it was discovered that she no longer believed herself to be the center of discussion. She gave the reason for her change of mind quite simply: "I could tell from the way they talked that they were completely wrapped up in their own thoughts and problems. You know, what you said about 'private worlds.' I realized that they weren't at all interested in me."

Returning to the man who believed himself pursued by

gangsters, it may be suspected that, in addition to the disturbance to clear thinking that results from acute anxiety, there was also a weakness in *knowledge of human motives*. This kind of weakness was touched on earlier, in the discussion of Marcella, the "outcast." In the present case it seems doubtful that fear alone would suffice to explain the exaggerated notions this patient had about the lengths to which his persecutors might go to revenge themselves. For example, that they would, for so minor an offense, pursue him from city to city, send a disguised agent to the hospital, etc. Owing to his unfortunate early life and the effect of his occupation upon close contacts with others, we may surmise that he failed to acquire adequate knowledge of the *ways in which people are moved to act*. Knowledge of this kind might have helped to check his delusional tendency with the thought: "This is foolish. People simply would not behave like that."

guilt and delusion

"Persecution behavior" very similar to that which may result from fear may also have its source in another emotional state. This is ordinarily called the feeling of guilt. There is, as we all know, a special kind of feeling which goes with consciousness of having done something which is socially disapproved, and which therefore gives rise to the experience of shame. This is true, at any rate, when the person himself accepts or agrees with the social judgment.

The case of the masturbating boy mentioned earlier would be one example of this kind of guilt feeling. If we suppose, now, that in his anxiety about possible discovery, he misinterprets comments or gestures as meaning that people have learned his secret and are about to accuse him, jeer at him or ostracize him, we see the beginnings of the connection between guilt and delusion. Possibly the boy may have been prepared for this kind of experience by way of the common belief that this practice leaves signs which others may read, like the girl who thought that it might change her walk, and who therefore became very seclusive, rarely appearing in public.

Just as the fearful person "sees" threats and dangers where they do not exist, so the guilty person "hears" accusations that have never been uttered. Perhaps the simplest form of this human tendency is seen in what is called self-consciousness. When one is, for some reason, highly aware of himself, he tends to think that others, too, are aware of him, like the boy with his first long trousers, or the girl with her first high heels.

The next case illustrates the extreme degree to which a person who has rejected himself through a judgment of guilt, may come to believe that others have adopted the same attitude toward him.

Gus

Gus is a rather pallid and pathetic looking boy of twenty-eight. He is of German descent. He is blond and blue-eyed; he has a narrow face, a long nose and a conspicuous "Adam's apple" set in a long, thin neck.

Everybody on his ward in the hospital likes Gus because he is so polite and deferential. He is self-effacing, and his characteristic expression is that of a person about to apologize for something. He often feels in the way, and for this reason is inclined to hold himself at a distance.

Gus was hospitalized by his parents because of an attempt at suicide, because he had been deeply depressed, and also because he felt that his family was trying to get rid of him. He had become suspicious of his food, and on one occasion accused his mother of wishing to poison him. There didn't seem to be much doubt that Gus had developed a persecution complex.

Fortunately he was a very intelligent boy, and it was possible to work out with him a fairly clear understanding of what had led up to his belief that he was worthless, must be punished, deserved to die, was to be killed, etc. During the period of his recovery he was able to recall how he felt when his thinking was becoming affected. "I sensed an antagonism. *I felt so inadequate I just thought the things they said and did were hostile when actually they were not.* For example, if they tried to give me a sedative I might think it was poison. It was simply my own feeling that my presence was no longer desirable."

The effects of strong feelings of self-rejection have been illustrated in other cases. But how explain the difference between the behavior of Gus and that, for example, of Marcella, who also felt rejected? We note, first, that while Marcella fought back angrily at what she felt was the contempt of her neighbors, Gus, apparently, had *accepted* what he felt was the judgment of others upon him. The impulse to retaliate was lacking (at least, by comparison). Gus, we might say, bowed to defeat, as Marcella would not.

How did Gus get this way? His docility seems to have gotten an early start. "I was always timid," he tells us; "I always felt that maybe I was taking up too much of somebody's time. I never had much self assertion. I depended a lot on what others thought. It was hard for me to take an independent stand."

As a boy Gus was highly conscious of his homely appearance. He was thin and knew that he was unattractive, awkward in movements, ungainly in posture. At school he studied hard; social activities were at a minimum. He made good grades, "but there was always the feeling that I should have done better. I guess I was always straining a bit, always sort of driving myself. I couldn't seem to relax. I couldn't watch a movie; I'd feel guilty. Recreation was always last on the list. My parents had the same tendency to frown on recreation."

The atmosphere of the home in which Gus and his younger brother were reared was sober. There was little or no gaiety. Gus says: "I was raised in a puritanical atmosphere . . . a straight and rigid home . . . we walked a straight and narrow path." The father was a hard worker, a "serious kind of person," who worried much about his health. Life was mainly a routine, with little play. The mother was a meticulous housewife, preoccupied with her own health and that of her children, much inclined to worry. "She was overly concerned about what people said. She was very sensitive to people, especially when they criticized. She was very cautious. She thought much about the serious side. There was never any joking or lightheartedness. She and I were alike in taking things pretty seriously. I guess my tendency to worry goes back many years; my oversensitiveness, too."

The outcome of such a background for a boy inclined, as was Gus, to be very submissive, is fairly well summed up in his own words: "I've always been too conscientious, yet I always felt inadequate, too. I guess that's why I was so sensitive to any criticism. I was often on the defensive, feeling I had to make an accounting for something. My standards were too high. I didn't give myself enough leeway."

Although Gus could not bring himself to say so directly, it was clear that his parents had been inclined, for a long while, to be domineering and over-critical. Timid as he was, the time came, finally, when Gus rebelled. The effort of control became too great, and impulses toward expression reached an explosive climax. There was a period of strong emotion, which Gus does not recall very well, as is often the case when feelings are intense. The details remain vague, but there were thwartings, disparagements and naggings by the parents, and then the moment when Gus became fully enraged. He finds it difficult to tell exactly what happened, and his discomfort under questioning is evident, but he does remember that in his extremity he screamed and was physically threatening toward his mother and father. Even now, he tells us, the awful echo of the words "I hate you" sometimes returns to torment him.

The aftermath of the rage was catastrophic. The enormity of his rebellion descended upon him like an avalanche. Overwhelmed with guilt and the agonizing conviction of unworthiness beyond redemption, his depression became suicidal. The certainty that he was no longer fit to live engulfed him, radiated outward upon others. From the assurance that he deserved to die it was but a step to the belief that he was about to be killed. The "persecutors" were, for Gus, not so much enemies from whom to flee, as the agents of a well-merited punishment.

Prominent during his stay in the hospital were expressions of guilt and unworthiness. Gus was sure he must be punished. Because of this feeling, and despite evidence of insight into his emotional problem, he was not able at any time to bring himself to speak critically of his parents. He became very uncomfortable when encouraged to discuss any resentment aroused by their treatment: "I just do not feel that they should be blamed for any of this." Gus understood the need of an emotion-free discussion of his relationship to his parents, but was quite unable to achieve this. The lifelong habits, reinforced by the guilt of his rebellion, were too strong. They continued to color his thinking and his perceptions of the feelings of others toward him.

the guilt conflict in a novelist

An extraordinary example of the linkage between guilt feeling and the persecution complex may be seen in the writings of Franz Kafka. Among this young man's novels and stories, now world famous, is a book that takes the reader directly and vividly into the strange-seeming world in which the "paranoid" lives. Part of Kafka's autobiographical writings provides an insight, moreover, into the meaning of this world. It tells plainly what may happen, in childhood and youth, to set the stage for tendencies of this kind.

Kafka's novel, *The Trial*,[4] opens with the arrest of the chief character, who is referred to as "K." The charge against him is not stated, and he does not know why he is under arrest. "Someone must have been telling lies about Joseph K . . ." He is allowed to go about his business, but receives a call to appear for questioning.

At the hearing room he finds an assembly of people. "K" takes the offensive and charges unfair treatment. Back of his arrest, he thinks, a "great organization" is at work. He sees the magistrate make a "secret sign" to someone in the audience. He notices that some of the onlookers are wearing badges, and concludes from this that they are in league with the magistrate, and have come to spy upon him.

Mental patients who talk of "organizations" against them, and who notice signs and signals among the persons they suspect, are well known to the staffs of psychiatric hospitals. Their vagueness regarding the motives of their persecutors, or of the charges against them, is frequently noted. Familiar also is the fact that "K" finds that various people whom he would have supposed were quite ignorant of his case, appear to be acquainted with it. Strangers seem to know about him, or even to have some kind of "connection" with his case.

Common also among paranoids is an interest in legal issues and in interpretations of the law, especially as it applies to their own situations. "K" becomes greatly preoccupied with details of the law, with pleas, defenses, lawyers and judgments. Kafka's prolonged discussion of such matters in his novel suggests an unusual personal interest in the various issues centering about a person who feels himself on trial and is filled with anxiety over the outcome of his case.

The most important feature of this story of "K" is the idea that *The Trial* is in reality a trial of self, that "K" is actually being tried by his own conscience. The guilt comes from a judgment within, more than by a charge from without. Thus, "K" says that it is a trial "only . . . if I recognize it as such." After his first visit to the "Court" he returns without being told to do so. There is no evidence of force, or mention of physical punishment or imprisonment, and "K" is allowed to go about his daily work unmolested. His case is a criminal one, but it "is not a case before an ordinary court." "K" feels that he could choose, himself, all the questions for his own examination. He considers, in planning his defense, giving an accounting of his entire life, with a moral scrutiny of every important item of conduct, since, to meet an accusation which is never defined, the whole of life must be reviewed and examined.

This strange trial of an unknown crime is also without justice and without an end. The High Court, "K" learns, is arbitrary and unpredictable. Since the defense counsel, no more than the defendant, knows what the accusation is, defense must obviously be difficult. The right of defense itself, we learn, is only tolerated; it is not even legally recognized. The bringing of a charge is, moreover, almost the same as a conviction, and "K" is told that he might as well appeal to a row of judges painted on canvas as to protest innocence before this court. A genuine acquittal is nearly unheard of. A judgment might appear to be an acquittal, but this may be followed by a second arrest, a second acquittal by a third arrest, and so on.

Such a narrative obviously lacks the quality of real experience. For many it may suggest an anxiety-filled dream. The theme of *The Trial* is not, however, of the mood of a fantasy. The anxiety is real, there is a sinister undertone, and the novel ends with the arrival of two callers, who conduct "K" to a place of execution. There they plunge a knife into his heart. Although still unenlightened as to his offense, "K" appears not unwilling to meet death.

What does so strangely puzzling a story mean, and what would lead anyone to become engrossed with such a plot, as Kafka certainly seems to have been? The suggestion is strong that there must have been a *personal motive* of some rather extraordinary kind to impel anyone to write in this way.

The whole of *The Trial* revolves around a shadowy presence in the background. This presence, the *"Court,"* is powerfully authoritative. It is utterly unreasonable and unpredictable. It is the focus of all of "K's" anxiety, and students of the novel have seen clearly that the "Court" is a symbol for Kafka's father. That the core of the emotional state which led him to write it—its inner meaning, in other words—was a painfully sharp and deep-seated guilt feeling in relation to his father, is suggested by a number of facts of Kafka's life, and most of all by his famous *Letter to His Father*.[5]

In this letter we learn what a father can do, unknowingly, to the spirit of a child. It tells how he became, in effect, an emotional cripple; how his morale was permanently shattered and a deep feeling of worthlessness was implanted through the blasting impact of his father's personality. The latter was vigorous, loud, dominating and successful, while little Franz seems to have been a timid and very sensitive child.

We are introduced to the central theme of *The Letter* in the brief account of a childish disobedience in which Franz was punished by being taken by his father, at night, to an outside balcony, and there abandoned. It was apparently an experience of desertion, terror and of not-understood rejection. It was a symbol of what led to the feeling of worthlessness which came finally to overwhelm him, and which he himself traced largely to his father's influence. It is clear that the boy was thoroughly over-awed by the parental authority whose shouts were a "heavenly commandment." He was repeatedly shamed and humiliated by his father's judgments. His thinking became dominated by the weight of this giant whose every ruling, no matter how contradictory or unreasonable, he felt must somehow be *right*, nevertheless, by the sheer power of its positiveness.

"For me," he writes, in this testament of protest and confession addressed to his father, "you took on the enigmatic quality that all tyrants have whose rights are based on their person, and not on reason." This belittling steadily undermined his morale: ". . . courage, resolution, confidence . . . did not endure . . . when you were against whatever it was or even if your opposition was merely to be assumed; and it was to be assumed in almost everything I did."

The idea, so prominent in Kafka's writings, of the unreasonableness of authority, in great part stems clearly from parental treatment: ". . . you . . . so tremendously the measure of all things for me, yourself did not keep the commandments you imposed on me." Kafka's mother, by being secretly protective and permissive, caused him to feel, before his father, "again the furtive creature, the cheat, the guilty one . . ."

So great was the father-authority that it became the supreme judgment in Kafka's own valuation of himself. Every effort to express his own personality led to anxiety. He writes: "I lost my self-confidence where you were concerned, and in its place . . . developed a boundless sense of guilt." The guilt included his friends as well, because "you always had some objection to make . . . to everyone I associated with, and for this too I had to beg his pardon."

Kafka's father was a self-made success; things had not been easy for him. Kafka's youth was much more comfortable, and it appears that he was not allowed to forget it. His father's comments on this had, he says, "worn grooves in my brain." He was belittled in other ways, and speaks of ". . . the suffering and shame you could inflict on me with your words and judgments." At times, made to feel at fault, he might be pardoned, with the result that "here again what accumulated was only a sense of guilt. On every side I was to blame . . ." There was guilt, too— it has been suggested—associated with his devotion to literary work, so much in contrast with his father's solidly successful business career. Major sources of guilt feeling, however, were the various weaknesses he compared with his father's strengths: ". . . this was the greatest disgrace of all."

Kafka's friend and chief biographer tried to help him, we are told, to see that his self-contempt was really groundless, and that his awe of his father was exaggerated, but the attempt failed. Kafka could not break free. His need of his father's acceptance was beyond reason. In his diaries we read: "Is not Father's power such that nothing (not I, certainly) could have resisted his decree?" [6]

Returning to *The Letter*, there is clear evidence of the emotional source, within the father-conflict, of certain of Kafka's productions. Referring to his books as a possible mark of true independence, he writes (to his father): "Of course it was a delusion: I was not . . . free. My writing was all about you . . ."

And again, concerning discussions with his sister, he explains that their purpose was to review "with all our might and main . . . in affection, defiance . . . submission, consciousness of guilt . . . *this terrible trial that is pending* between us and you, to discuss it in all its details, from all sides, on all occasions . . . *a trial in which you keep on claiming to be the judge.*"

The preoccupation with guilt and punishment is repeated in another of Kafka's principal novels, *The Castle.*[7] The heroine, Amalia, asserts her independence by rejecting an insulting advance by a person of power. Though the advance is an abuse of authority, and without justice, Amalia's offense is considered unpardonable. She is despised by all, her family shamed and ruined. There follows a prolonged, anxious *appeal to authority for release from the burden of guilt.* Yet this authority can "only condemn and not pardon." There is, in the entire novel, a great awe of authority symbols, a great amount of mulling over ways and means of approaching them, and a marked indirection, one might say a *shyness,* in making such approaches.

The tyranny and inescapable power of the father-image is seen again in the short story significantly named *The Judgment.*[8] It describes a brief verbal conflict between a father and son. It begins on a casual note, a discussion of the son's approaching marriage. Then, without visible motive, the father's tone changes. He becomes accusing, challenging, charges his son with wickedness, with an attempt to seize power. He ridicules, proclaims his dominance. The son is frightened and cowed. The father then makes "the judgment": death by drowning. Immediately, and without protest, the son leaps to his death.

Here the father symbol stands for authority without reason or justice. It is sinister and overpowering. The judgment is accepted as absolute, the atonement swift and unquestioning, as if impelled by overwhelming guilt.

In the short story, *The Penal Colony,* the theme of condemnation, punishment and atonement appears again. The condemned man does not know his offense, but he has broken the law: "Honor your superior." The guiding principle in such cases is that guilt is never doubtful. The instrument of punishment is a complex torture machine which is described in great detail. By prolonged suffering the victims experience a spiritual redemption. This story reads like a literary expression of its author's emotional conflict. Just as a resentful person may indulge in imaginary revenge, and a sex-hungry person in imaginary gratifications, so one burdened with guilt might seek relief in a fantasy of condemnation, and of suffering which leads to pardon.

Kafka's writings, along with some of the facts about his life, suggest some important conclusions for the understanding of the persecution complex.

First, that an emotional relationship with a parent or parents may have, in some individuals, a lasting, profound and dominating effect upon personality.

Again, that when this conflict involves strong feelings of guilt as a response to accusation, humiliation and belittling, the resulting emotional wound may express in thoughts and feelings having to do with persecutions and persecutors, in preoccupation with "trials," "judgments," charges and defenses, punishment, rejection and atonement, etc.

Finally, there is evidence that the full meaning of some of his stories was not clear to Kafka himself at the time of writing. This parallels the fact that such conflicts may be unconscious, in part or entirely; that the true paranoid may fail—typically does fail—to comprehend the meaning of his conviction that there are forces moving against him, that accusing fingers are pointing in his direction.

anger and delusion

The manner in which strong feelings may twist our ways of perceiving and of believing into the disorders called delusions has been illustrated for the emotion of fear and for the sense of guilt. What of anger?

It is a commonplace that we are inclined to believe unfavorable things of people we dislike. Closely related is the tendency to believe that which offers an excuse (called a "reason") for the release of hostile feeling against another. In an earlier chapter we cited the small boy who vengefully gave false reports of another lad toward whom he felt resentful. Another example would be that of the eight-year-old who, jealous of the new baseball glove of a playmate, tried to start the rumor going that "His mother stole it."

The delusions of the mentally disordered often contain absurdities, it is true, but here again there are parallels with experiences familiar to most of us. Anyone who has ever, through fear, momentarily given credence to a far-fetched possibility, later seen as highly unreal but accepted at the time, has known what emotion can do to one's ability to see facts as they are. By the same token, anyone who, in the midst of a bitter resentment, has made an accusation at least half-believed at the moment he made it, yet easily recognized as groundless when calm returned, has glimpsed within himself the mental workings which play a part in the delusions traceable to strong feelings.

Returning for a moment to the case of Marcella, it was seen that her thinking was very strongly affected by her emotions. Her resentment arose, at every thought of her neighbors, to a pitch that caused her to believe things of them which were absurdly untrue. Since, while at home, her neighbors were on her mind much of the time, her hostile mood was, under these conditions, almost constant. At other times, Marcella could be a calm and friendly person. This was true throughout her interviews at the hospital, and in her contacts with other patients. It was, for the most part, only within the setting of her community, where she felt that social acceptance was denied her, that her disorder was evident.

These features of Marcella's case have been reviewed in order to introduce another in which will be seen, not only a more continuous and extreme expression of hostility, but a more marked degree of the kind of delusional thinking that may result from this emotion.

Ada

Ada is a tall, rather thin, black-haired woman of 38. She is unmarried, and has been living with her mother while employed as a bookkeeper. Although not pretty, Ada's features would be pleasant enough were it not for her habitually sullen expression.

Ada, like Marcella, was hospitalized because of "neighbor trouble." She was persistently bothered by "peddlers, boys, children ringing doorbells." Sometimes Ada felt that her neighbors were trying to get her to leave the neighborhood. "They watched every move I made," she complained; "maybe they think I'm queer or funny-looking." Ada became increasingly hostile. Among other symptoms, she suspected that there might be poison in her food. She charged that the neighbors entered the house in her absence. Once, in a rage, she destroyed some furniture, and it was necessary to call in a family friend to subdue her. Finally, Ada remarked that she would kill certain people if she had a gun. At this, the family physician advised that she be brought to the hospital.

During her stay, Ada's behavior might have been called a prolonged sulk, with occasional mild outbursts of irritability. Her tone was resentful and challenging, often sarcastic. While taking psychological tests it was noted that she often seemed to be doing her best to be contrary. She sought opportunities to contradict. When asked, for example, among other questions on an intelligence test, why it is better to build a house out of brick than of wood, she replied that this was not true, that wood was better because brick would crumble, that a brick house was too heavy for its foundations, etc. She refused to retract any statement once made, or to admit an error, and would deny the most obvious common sense or try to defend very poor logic rather than admit that she could be wrong.

When facts were suggested which did not agree with her views, she rejected them with a note of angry challenge. In answer to some personal questions she deliberately falsified some of her replies, sometimes quite pointlessly, in sheer release of hostility. At another time, with a more pointed motive, she denied the existence of a sister ("I haven't got any sisters") toward whom she felt resentful. Ada's tone and expression on these occasions conveyed an intensely hostile feeling, and this was also evident when she made certain charges against her neighbors. One of these was that they deliberately sent their children to bother her, under pretense of playing near her home; they were noisy, destroyed flowers, etc.

Another charge was that an "abortion racket" was being carried on in a nearby house. Ada waxed indignant as well as bitter about this. A little questioning revealed that she had read some newspaper reports about such "rackets." She had also seen strange young women, on different occasions, enter the home of the neighbor. Ada therefore "put two and two together," and denied with heat that this was hardly adequate grounds for so serious an accusation.

Did Ada know what she was doing when she made such charges? Was she consciously falsifying, as a way of venting her anger? These questions have been encountered before. They are important because they are tied up with the difference between being delusional—that is, being mentally ill—and being essentially a normal person, yet capable of allowing one's thinking to be colored and distorted, from time to time, by emotional states.

An angry person, as we all know, may say things he afterwards realizes are untrue, and he may recognize that he said them *because* he was angry, and not because they were true. He may even realize that he *believed* what he said at the time he said it; that is, at the moment of his emotion. We could say, then, that he was "temporarily delusional" (in a sense somewhat similar, perhaps, to that of the popular reference to a person in extreme rage as "temporarily insane").

The important difference is that in the one instance the "delusion" vanishes as the emotion subsides, while in a case such as that of Ada, false beliefs about her neighbors were steadily supported by continuous hostility. Since her feelings were unaltered —that is, since her mood did not subside—the belief persisted, and Ada was said to exhibit "fixed ideas" about these people. Her feelings were, moreover, constantly in evidence. Not once during the period of many months of hospitalization did her mood break. The bitterness was sustained, as if what might have been a single moment of feeling had been somehow frozen into a permanent emotional "posture," like those tricks of the movies in which time is supposed to stand still, and the behavior of an instant is perpetuated for minutes or hours.

Anger, then, like fear and like guilt, may lead to false beliefs. It can be far more than the passing spasm of familiar experience, and more even than a mood of hours and days. It can become a fixed hostility that may endure for years, and thereby provide a steady support for equally enduring false beliefs. Moreover, despite the impression one might get that Ada's delusions were deliberate falsifications, there is no more need to doubt her sincerity than in other cases considered in which similar beliefs were rooted in strong emotion.

In the case of Willie, the angry boy described in Chapter 4, hostility was seen as affecting the whole of behavior, and in a variety of ways altering the quality of personality, yet without giving rise to any real delusional thinking. In Marcella's case the major delusions were a product of her habitual feeling of rejection, though some of them appeared to express her resentment. Her hostility was for the most part limited, however, to her immediate neighbors; with others she could be quite amiable and mild mannered. In Ada, finally, hostility appears in fully matured bloom. It not only sustained her delusions but was manifested in nearly everything she did. No occasion was too small to serve as a release for some bitterness. It showed in her face, her manner, her tone and in her social withdrawal.

What was the matter with Ada, and whence came the sharp and impartial antagonisms that poisoned her feeling for others,

and led finally to a mental hospital? By this time, and after
Willie's and Marcella's cases, the reader will doubtless know what
to expect.

Ada's chronic emotional state was an effective bar to deeper
exploration. She was in no mood for confessions, or for any calm
consideration of her attitude toward people. However, when
questioned under the influence of a relaxing drug whose purpose
was to allow expression to blocked-off feelings, she revealed a
part of herself which made clear the true nature of her emotional
disturbance. Ada began to talk in a way she had not talked before. Although her thoughts tended to be somewhat disconnected,
they came spontaneously and in a fairly continuous stream.

Among the many thoughts and feelings revealed at this time,
a few may be quoted which enlighten the sources of Ada's resentment. "I'm not comfortable with people," she confessed; "it's
my personality. I've been terribly lonesome. . . . Yes, I could
have misunderstood my neighbors. I'm wrapped up in myself.
My neighbors are all right. It's me. I'm queer. I like people but
they don't like me. They don't take to me. . . . I'm a failure. I
should never have been born. I'm a burden to others."

Here, again, beneath the surface appearance of hardened
aloofness, was a person who had suffered the painful hurt of personal rebuff, who had never been sure of herself, never able to
feel that she was fully accepted. It was further apparent that the
basic anger was directed against herself; she was "queer," a burden, a failure. In its usual expression, however, the anger was discharged outwardly and blindly, in an exasperated and futile striking out, as when she falsified facts and challenged the obvious.

Why did Ada believe herself persecuted? One who is angered by rejection is in an awkward position. He can hardly admit, at least not without a touch of shame, the true source of his
resentment. A child might confess: "I don't like them because
they don't like me," but for an adult this is too plainly a confession of inadequacy, and too hard on one's pride. It is much easier
to seek excuses for venting one's spleen upon others. The logic
then becomes: "I don't like them (not because they don't like

me) because they are saying and doing things against me (I don't know why)."

Some of Ada's accusations simply reflected the meaning she gave to incidents. For example, the neighbors' children annoyed her *on purpose*. (Anyone who, if only for a moment of irritable exasperation, has believed that events were *intentionally* opposing his efforts, has had a glimpse of this state of mind.) There were other accusations which went beyond this, however, and seemed to verge on pure fabrication.

In short, Ada needed to believe her charges were true to give vent to her resentful anger. She needed this belief to justify her resentment. Without it, her humiliation would have been too painful to bear.

something to hide: delusions as defense

Three different ways in which the persecution complex may arise as the effect of an emotional state have been considered. In these cases a strong emotion leads directly to misreadings of the behavior of others.

Some instances may now be described in which a false belief is an attempt to protect the self from a humiliating admission of some sort. Here one believes falsely, not from fear, or guilt or anger, but to escape from painful feelings, usually those which result from conflicts involving pride or social censure.

The supposed motive of the persecutors need not always be unfriendly in the usual sense. It might even be considered as rather flattering. A girl of twelve was observed to complain to her friends that a neighborhood boy was annoying her by "hanging around" her. She made unfavorable comments about his appearance and deportment. At times she dwelled at considerable length upon certain characteristics of his which she claimed to dislike. Finally, a discerning member of the girl's own coterie remarked, "You certainly seem to have him on your mind a lot. I think you must really have a crush on him." At this the girl be-

came quite emotional, denying the charge with so much ve-
hemence that her reaction struck her friends as exaggerated and
somewhat puzzling.

The girl was in reality attracted to the boy. Attraction to
neighborhood boys was not, however—at her age and among
her crowd—either approved or accepted. She could not admit
her feelings to her friends, and it is likely that she could not fully
admit them to herself. The truth of the matter was that it was she
who had been, to some degree, "hanging around" the boy. In
order to protect herself and to divert attention, she felt that she
must charge him with responsibility for being seen near her. Her
behavior was a way of saying: "It is not I who am attracted; it is
he." Her unfavorable comments served the purpose of a further
denial that there was anything about him that appealed to her.
She had unknowingly, perhaps, adopted the old principle that a
good way to defend yourself is to take the offensive.

The same kind of experience can happen, at the opposite
end of the age scale, to an elderly unmarried woman who suddenly begins to complain of the undesirable attentions to which
she is subjected by some male acquaintance. First she thinks he
wants to marry her, and later she believes he is about to abduct
her forcibly; she may react by writing him an indignant letter or
lodging a complaint with the police, who find in their investigation that the man not only is entirely innocent of the charges
but may even be only dimly aware of the old woman's existence.
Whereupon the lady is certified to be suffering from "delusions
of persecution" and is removed to a hospital.

Obviously she misunderstood the man's intentions. In most
cases of this type, the reason usually is that the old woman cannot
admit to herself the presence of sexual desire on her part, probably because of a prudish upbringing and her long life alone.
Unwilling or unable to understand her strong attraction to a
relative stranger, she deceives herself by reversing the attraction
in her mind; thus the stranger suddenly becomes predatory.

Nearly everyone has experienced, at one time or another, the
kind of defensive impulse illustrated here, though the situation

might be an entirely different one. When one is faced with a humiliating blunder or with a weakness of character, sheer denial that it exists may not succeed. It must therefore be explained, to one's self, if not to others. If someone else may be charged, fairly or not, with some part of the blame, our distress will be eased.

Among familiar examples is the student who assigns to his teacher partial responsibility for his poor grades (for example, because of personal dislike, unfair questions, unjust grading system, and so on), or the man who, failing to get a promotion because of incompetence, accuses his superiors of favoritism, "office politics," or ignorance of his abilities.

Examples of such defensive maneuvers among the mentally ill were illustrated earlier. It would be easy to arrange a series of examples ranging from the normal to such extremes as that of the highly moralistic patient who blamed his enemies for causing his head to turn, by some kind of "electronic" device, to follow the seductive figure of a feminine passerby. They also caused him to have sensations in his genitals and the impulse to masturbate. By thus using his body, he explained, they obtained gratification for themselves: "Whenever I have sensations of this kind, they are duplicated by sensations in the people who cause me to have them." A female patient, similarly, believed that someone had controlled her hand in the act of masturbating, and that "somebody was trying to make my knees fall apart, like a prostitute; my knees were going apart like somebody was moving them—not myself."

An interesting expression of homosexual inclinations has been studied by the psychoanalytic school. Suppose that a youth's attraction to his own sex is so repugnant to his moral ideas or to his standards of masculinity that he cannot acknowledge it. He finds himself emotionally disturbed in the presence of a certain man. Because he cannot recognize or accept this experience for what it is, he is forced to make the familiar shift ("It is not I, it is he") and to regard the man as a persecutor. The latter, by reason of his emotional effect, comes to *stand for* the forbidden inclination, and the youth is in reality "persecuted" by his own rejected impulses. And like the young girl who was "bothered" by the boy, the youth made another the offender. Again, just as the girl expressed dislike for the boy, the youth "hates" the one whom, in reality, he loves.

At a cocktail party a young married woman was observed to be displaying enough interest in one of the male guests to justify some degree of jealous irritation on the part of her husband. He himself had expressed little more than conventional interest in a young woman with whom he had casually engaged in conversation. When, alone with his wife at the party's end, he was about to berate her for unseemly behavior, he was disconcerted and thrown out of stride by her heated accusation that *he* had been far too attentive to his companion to please *her*.

Such defensive devices as these are by no means limited to the guilt feelings so often linked with sex. There are, obviously, many other ways in which a person may feel disapproved, unworthy, or self-rejected. Marcella certainly had a persecution complex, but this had its roots in experiences unrelated to sex. In a variety of human relationships we could find examples of the familiar formula that one of the best ways to defend one's self is to take the offensive. It not only points the blame elsewhere for the benefit of onlookers, but protects the pointer's own self-esteem if he can manage to deceive himself as well.

Four different ways in which people may come to feel threatened by others have been considered. It should be clear that the disorders grouped under the persecution complex are not all alike in source. The term applies to a variety of behavior problems. The fear that one is being pursued by a lover is far different from the fear that one is to be punished for worthlessness or for misdeeds. To believe that one has been wronged, as an excuse for venting resentment, is very different from believing that one has been victimized by people jealous of one's abilities. And all of these are different from a fear that, beginning with some degree of real danger, magnifies it, by compounding false interpretations into an enormous threat.

The belief that people are in some way unfriendly or hostile is the most widely prevalent form of delusional disorder. Why should mental disturbance so often take this form? It has been suggested that the age and the society in which we live offers an abundance of situations in which fear, hostility, guilt and feelings of unworthiness may be aroused. The influences that threaten security are more numerous than those that help to support it. These influences may affect certain individuals so sharply, and may lodge their effects so deeply, as to leave serious and lasting damage to the emotional life and to the personality.

delusion
① fear
② guilt
③ anger
} misreading, misinterpretation of the behavior of others.

④ defense — to protect self from painful feelings

6. a famous

schizophrenic

All or most of us are moved to defend ourselves as best we can against charges of weakness and inadequacy. We tend, likewise, to avoid admitting such defects to ourselves as well as to others. It is, as everyone knows, the need to support self-esteem and to escape humiliation that lies behind such efforts at defense.

Usually the measures that must be taken for this purpose are not extraordinary. With moderate degrees of pride and in the face of moderate demands upon defense resources, nothing unusual in the way of alibis, excuses and shifts of blame is needed. These devices will have, moreover, a fair plausibility. In the run-of-the-mill case, pride will not be extreme, the failure not too painful, the problem not exceptional, and nothing farfetched required to provide a way out. When a man blames the failure of a poorly planned business venture on bad luck or adverse circumstances, or a bad tennis game on a sore wrist or a poor racket, it may be seen as routine defensive behavior, normal, and in some degree just about universal.

But what happens, or may happen, if the conflict is an extremely painful one because pride is extraordinarily intense and sensitive, and because a weakness or inadequacy happens to be of an exceptionally humiliating character? Suppose also that in this agonizing distress the situation is such that no realistic or plausible escape can be made.

As a preliminary exercise in understanding the possibilities

92

in such a situation, a case reported from the literature on mental illness may be considered.

It is that of a man who has been hospitalized for a long time because of some rather weird ideas. He thinks that certain persecutors, by exerting extraordinary influence upon him, are causing him to be tormented with sexual sensations and feelings which he finds, or professes to find, revolting. The "influences" by which this is achieved are invisible, and act over long distances. Of main interest here is the kind of experience that could lead to such a disorder, and the kind of person to whom it could happen.

Important, first of all, is a particular *build* of personality. The man is described, at the outset, as exaggerated in his self-esteem, confident to the point of arrogance. In the midst of his exalted pretensions and a feeling of contemptuous superiority toward others, he now discovers within himself, not only that he is timid and inadequate in the region of sexual behavior, but that he has a natural disposition toward effeminacy.

In a society such as ours, in which "real manhood" is so closely linked with sex virility and masculine courage, such a discovery might well be catastrophic, especially to a person who tends strongly toward vanity. It may easily be believed that the conflict was completely unbearable. Here, where the most exalted ego was confronted with the most degrading and shameful defect, is something approaching the ultimate degree of human internal crisis. The effect of directly facing the facts would be like an explosion in a locked room.

That such a person should begin to feel himself regarded as an object of contempt is understandable enough; likewise that the onset of his disorder should show the familiar mistaken interpretations of remarks in which he finds the accusation that he is queer and lacking in masculinity.

In the next phase the idea develops that he has become the object of a plot in which certain evil persons (through motives which need not be detailed) are causing him, or forcing him, to experience the emotions, thoughts and desires of a woman. The

extraordinary means by which these influences are exerted, he believes, involve not only supernatural forces, but also electrical
action, in which the nerves of his skin are likened to "tiny radio
antennae capable of receiving sensations."

While the delusional system here includes some rather
strange notions, to be later considered, its meaning is clear
enough. Through the belief that *others* are working these criminal
effects upon him, he is able to enjoy otherwise forbidden and
shameful erotic sensations and emotions with the excuse that he
is a passive and helpless victim. Feminine feelings, homosexual
desires, the impulse to masturbate, all now become tolerable since
full responsibility can be charged to the persecutors. The delusions are thus, in effect, a denial of ownership. The patient has
"pointed the finger" elsewhere. He has made the *paranoid shift.*

We are now ready to consider in more detail a similar case,
famous in the literature of mental illness. Here the story comes to
us directly from the patient's own account of his experience.

the case of Schreber

The mental disorder of Daniel Paul Schreber has become
"the most quoted case in psychiatry" partly because he wrote
at great length about his experience, and, being unusually well
educated, he was able to write very well about it. Perhaps more
important, a study of Schreber by Sigmund Freud became much
better known than Schreber's own *Memoirs of My Nervous Illness.*[1]

Schreber's family was prominent; his father was a physician
with a number of books to his credit. A great-uncle was re-
nowned as a scientist, was a Fellow of the Royal Society of London. Schreber entered the legal profession and in his early fifties
had reached a high office; he was a jurist, president of an appel-
late court with supreme jurisdiction over a kingdom (Saxony) of
some five million people. He was described as a man of wide and
varied intellectual interests, being well read in science, history,

philosophy and religion as well as in public affairs. His honesty was reputed to be beyond reproach.

The "nervous illness," as Schreber called it in the book he wrote about it, led to nearly ten years of hospitalization. He kept notes during his illness, near the end of this period, and began his book in anticipation of his discharge and return to society. Its purpose was, in part, to call the attention of men of science to a unique phenomenon, namely, that his body was being changed into that of a woman. It was also to explain why he might frequently be seen wearing feminine ornaments.

Schreber attributed his illness to strain from overwork. He became sleepless, had attacks of anxiety and depression, and was finally removed to a hospital where he became delusional and hallucinated.

In his detailed account of his experience, a number of different trends, or themes, are evident. The idea of a change of sex was but one of these. The selection of this symptom for illustrative purposes represents, therefore, a simplification of the case as a whole. Some other factors which may have been at work will be briefly noted in the proper place.

Central among Schreber's delusions was his conviction that he had a mission, and that this mission was the redemption of the world. Among the phenomena of mental illness, belief in this particular kind of personal destiny is not rare, but in Schreber's case it took a distinctive form. He believed that in order for his mission to be completed it was essential that he first be *transformed into a woman*. In this transformation, moreover, he was, he believed, but an instrument of the divine will. It was his inescapable fate to be so changed, by "imperious demand," much as he would have preferred to retain his manliness. It became his "right and duty," therefore, to cultivate femininity. Having thus no choice, he "wholeheartedly" accepted this fate, even though it might mean renouncing his profession and all other manly pursuits.

The miraculous change was actually taking place, he was convinced, in the form of alterations of his body. Not only did he habitually imagine feminine contours as taking shape; close scrutiny would convince an observer, he was sure, that there was a visible periodic swelling of his bosom. Anyone who saw the unclothed upper portion of his body would not, he thought, doubt its feminine character, this being especially true when he wore feminine adornments.

The process of conversion involved, among other things, the withdrawal of the male sex organs into the body. This change was to come about slowly; it might require several years. He had, he tells us, twice experienced the presence of a female genital organ; the miracle being "reversed" afterward, however. His skin had become softened, thus more feminine; more important, female "nerves of voluptuousness" developed in his body. They were present in every part, and he could feel them by pressing upon his skin, particularly upon his chest. Such pressure provided a feeling of sensuous pleasure, especially if he *thought* of something feminine.

Schreber refers repeatedly to these "nerves of voluptuousness." His treatment in the hospital at times confirmed his belief about what his destiny was to be. To encourage voluptuous sensations he was kept in bed, naked; medicines were forced upon him for the same purpose. The medical report on his behavior informs us, however, that Schreber found pleasure in feminine occupations and toilet articles and in viewing himself in a mirror in partial undress. He decorated himself with ribbons and bows. In a "low-cut vest," he gazed "at what he believes his female bosom."

As to the purpose of this transformation, two different themes appear in the *Memoirs*. According to one, the aim of his sexual transformation is the creation, by way of his own impregnation by God, of new human beings. He has, in fact, he tells us, already known the experience of "quickening" as, miraculously, the germ of new life has been implanted in his body.

Elsewhere in his account, however, Schreber hints of a different outcome. He speaks of his transformed body being abandoned to someone for the purpose of sexual abuse, "in the manner of a female harlot." There is suggested the familiar distinction between sex viewed in its basic and more "moral" aspect as a reproductive act, and sex in its more sensual or "lustful" aspect. The difference, in other words, between procreation and recreation. The point will be further developed.

The belief, then, in an adult male, that he is undergoing a change of sex by divine edict, and that he has been chosen for this purpose so that, by a kind of immaculate conception, the human race may be renewed, is our case material here. Few would ask more than this, doubtless, to judge a person mentally ill. It remains now to discover what such strange ideas mean in terms of the interpretations which have so far helped toward an understanding of this illness. Will we find here another instance, perhaps, of the "paranoid shift"?

Certain features of Schreber's personality are important. He was, as earlier mentioned, a jurist of high repute, and a community pillar whose behavior in general must have been well beyond reproach. His upbringing seems to have been in keeping with the social position he finally achieved. "Few people," he tells us, "have been brought up according to such strict moral principles as I, and have throughout life practiced such moderation especially in matters of sex. . . ." Those who have known him from early life would testify, he thinks, that he has been of calm nature, "without passion," "sober," "cool."

Notable in the *Memoirs* is evidence that to Schreber the conventional model of what constitutes the masculine ideal meant a great deal. References to masculinity and "manliness" are frequent, and there is repeated use of such expressions as manly pride, manly honor, manly courage, manly ambition, the sense of manliness, etc.

A certain attitude toward sex in its sensual aspect is also apparent. Sensuousness is "low"; in referring to the stimulation of voluptuous sensations Schreber uses the term "abominable"; his "entire moral being" revolts against it. He assures us that, if there is in his *Memoirs* a considerable discussion of sex matters, it is not due to "taste or predilection" on his part, but rather "entirely" to the fact that sexual matters have been stressed by the external influences which have been brought to bear upon him. He finds no pleasure in vulgarities; he emphasized the "moral seriousness" that pervades his writing about his illness.

On the whole, the picture is that of what is commonly termed a "high-minded" person, possibly rather rigid in his views of sex morals, strict in his interpretation of what is manly. He is inclined to reject sex in its sensual side, and probably tends to think of it as fully acceptable only as a means to procreation. We must remember, too, the period in which his illness developed. It was the nineties of the last century, a time hardly famed for a liberal philosophy of sex.

Schreber's account may now be examined to see if, in every respect, the experiences he reports during his illness are well fitted to the picture outlined. Of particular interest is his belief that the sole purpose of his conversion into a woman is the creation, divinely ordained, of new human beings, and that the sacrifice of his manhood is a demand made upon him in disregard of his own wishes.

There is, among other things, much talk of "voluptuousness," and also, as earlier mentioned, the idea that a secondary motive for the sexual transformation is that Schreber's female body is to be prostituted for sexual misuse. He seems to have engaged in a considerable amount of sexual fantasy: ". . . when I am lying in bed at night I can give myself . . . the impression that my body has female breasts and a female sexual organ." Imagining his buttocks are female in form has become a habit. Voluptuous feeling becomes at times "so strong that especially when I am in bed, it requires only a little exertion of my imagination to attain such sensuous pleasures as gives a pretty definite foretaste of female sexual enjoyment in intercourse." There are times when he must "strive to give . . . the impression of a woman in the height of sexual delight," to achieve which he must "strain his imagination."

Such candid revelations as this place the matter in a quite different light. Whatever needs led to Schreber's belief in his call to create a new race by divine impregnation, it is clear that there was something else at work of a far different order, and something moreover, which to a man of Schreber's standards would be of a very repugnant nature. It would look as if, in his disorganized state, some sexual impulses were coming to light, or being exposed, which ordinarily would be sharply in conflict with his highly moral attitudes. It begins to look, in fact, as if this dignified and "passionless" jurist not only has a genuinely passionate sexual nature, but that he might be one of those males whose sexual make-up includes, along with normal impulses, an ingredient of the feelings and inclinations of the opposite sex.

What could happen to a man of culture, strictly raised in an age of straight-laced standards of conduct, having a prominent position in public life and a conventional attitude with regard to masculinity as well as to sex, who discovers within himself impulses not only "carnal" but "perverted"?

In an earlier chapter an effort was made to show that when the mind discovers an impulse or feeling that is painfully at variance with standards or ideals, the conflict may be relieved by a refusal to *own* the impulse or the feeling, and by *shifting* the ownership—so to speak—to another person or to circumstances, according to the formula previously illustrated ("It is not I, it is he"; "They made me do it," etc.).

Did Schreber try to do this, and if so, how does it show in his confessions?

It is noted first, that as mentioned, he claims to have no choice in the matter of his conversion into a woman. Nothing is left but for him to reconcile himself. Not only this, but even the cultivation of voluptuousness is not his inclination but his duty. This kind of behavior has been forced upon him through his special relationship to God. Schreber borrows a term from the early Crusaders: "God wills it." God "demands" voluptuousness of him. The term "duty" occurs repeatedly in connection with the encouragement, within himself, of feminine feelings. It is "all for God" that he must do it, though he acknowledges the thought, at one point (and rather pathetically), that if he can get for himself "a little sensuous pleasure," he feels that he deserves this in reward for the trials and privations he has had to endure. At another place he shifts again, and says that he is "compelled" to produce "female sensuous pleasure" by stroking his body in order to induce sleep, but also that he feels entitled to seek relaxation for intellectual labor through voluptuousness. He gets "female sensuous pleasure" by way of pressure upon the "nerves of voluptuousness" in his chest region, but he assures us that he does this ("by the way") not to obtain sensual gratification but only because "absolutely compelled" to do it in order to induce sleep.

Further evidence as to the true character of the voluptuousness appears in Schreber's remark that this kind of enjoyment is ordinarily granted to human beings solely for reproductive purposes. Sensual pleasure carried beyond this goal would make man unfit for higher mental and moral activities. He emphasizes, however, that for *him* this rule does not apply; that, in fact, for him it is reversed, since it is his actual obligation to encourage sensual pleasure in himself, and that the special kind of sexual excitement which is his duty "under other circumstances might be considered immoral."

It is clear that Schreber justifies his sexual behavior, in the main, through his belief that he is under divine compulsion. He strengthens his defense still further by striving in various ways to exalt voluptuousness beyond its status as "mere low sensuousness." It is of much higher grade than this; it is, in fact, to be called "soul" voluptuousness, an expression which frequently recurs in Schreber's account. He thinks, moreover, that there is a close relation between this kind of experience and what he calls "blessedness." This is continuous enjoyment linked with the contemplation of God, but in the *female* it means continuous voluptuousness. Blessedness is felt as greatly increased pleasure of this kind. Schreber thus links "soul voluptuousness" on the one hand with feminine sexual enjoyment, and on the other with the blessedness enjoyed everlastingly by souls in Heaven. Thus does he bring sexual pleasure more and more within the odor of sanctity. He is, unconsciously, making "vice" virtuous.

He continues still further with this, or rather, it is carried further for him, for the divine voice explicitly encourages him in his pursuit of such pleasures. "Voluptuousness has become God-fearing," it tells him, and he is thus quite frankly enjoined to excite himself sexually. "Clearly," he states, "the usual ideas of morality have been reversed in my relation to God." The conflict is not wholly stilled, however, and other voices are heard. These are voices which we may take to express (as did Florrie's) the yet unreconciled remnants of conscience. They address themselves, as we might expect, to his "manly honor" when the voluptuous mood is upon him. They ask him if he is not ashamed before his wife, and, more vulgarly: "Fancy a person who was a (Senate-president) allowing himself to be f - - - - d."

To sum up, our view of Schreber's disorder is that during a period of nervous exhaustion by overwork, a previously repressed part of his sexual make-up, not only sensual but essentially feminine, forced its way upon his consciousness. Because of his rigid moral character this breakthrough was intolerable, and reconciliation was possible only by way of the conviction that a change-over in sex was divinely ordained for him, that his sensual feelings were therefore, and by special dispensation, acceptable to God.

Schreber writes that, before his illness, he had a highly peculiar experience. One morning while in bed, and probably only partially awake, it occurred to him that "it really must be rather pleasant to be a woman succumbing to intercourse." "This idea," he continues, "was so foreign to my whole nature that I may say I would have rejected it with indignation if fully awake; from what I have experienced since I cannot exclude the possibility that some external influences were at work to implant this idea in me."

Here we have, in Schreber's own words, in a nutshell, the central meaning of his illness: the unacceptable sexual thoughts, so foreign to his character, and the *disowning* of these thoughts by way of the surmise that they must have some source other than his own nature. Realization of their true meaning, in a man of

Schreber's standards and morals, would have meant an acute moral catastrophe.

The delusions in mental disorder may be so plausible in substance that only by investigation can it be certified that the patient is reporting a mistaken interpretation, rather than fact. Contrasting sharply with these are such productions as that of Schreber—and a great variety of comparable ones—so unrealistic in content as to be recognizable at a glance as the expression of a disordered mind. The "bizarre" delusion is, in fact, often seen as marking a more profound degree of illness.

It may be noted, however, that the character of a delusion may be largely *forced* by the nature of the patient's problem. There is no way of disowning one's bodily sensations except by making some rather remarkable assumptions. The patient had little choice but to talk of supernatural events, magnetic, electrical, or "mental" influences, or similar weird-sounding fabrications. His problem is such that the delusional solution must necessarily be far-fetched, if he is to have a solution at all.

That some of his beliefs were very gratifying to Schreber's ego can hardly be doubted. He is unique, the "greatest seer" who ever lived. The entire relationship between God and the whole of humanity rests upon His connection with Schreber, who at one point questions what is to become of God should he (Schreber) die! The continuation of all life on earth depends on him in his relation to God. "He maintains," his physician reported, "that he is the exclusive object of divine miracles, and the most remarkable human being that ever lived on earth."

The delusional disorders so far illustrated have been of two types: those in which the delusional interpretation is a direct expression of an emotional state, as anxiety, and those in which it is a defense against painful emotion. Schreber's symptom was clearly defensive in character, and shows how a delusion may provide a way out of an otherwise insoluble conflict. It also indicates another feature of such beliefs, namely, that they may provide direct satisfaction of certain urges—for example, the desire to feel important.

The *Memoirs* are rich in material for interpretation, and other points of view have been taken. Schreber's illness has been seen as the consequence of his frustration in having no children. The central delusion was motivated by the need to procreate; Schreber wanted, above all, to be able to reproduce.

According to Freud, the prime cause of Schreber's illness was an outbreak of homosexual desire for his physician. The latter came to be seen, therefore, as a persecutor. Unable, however, to reconcile himself to such a relationship (i.e., the role of "female prostitute" to his physician) the figure of God was substituted, since "the task of providing God himself with voluptuous sensations" aroused less resistance. The feminine fantasy had its real roots in an erotic desire for his own father, and Schreber's attitude toward God, as seen in his delusion, reflects his attitude toward his father.

The case is thus seen by Freud as essentially an expression of the "father complex"; it reproduces the infantile conflict with the father. Schreber's major delusion represented, according to Freud, a triumph of infantile sexuality; the parental threat (represented by God) of castration provided the motive for his wish to be changed into a woman.*

The case is a complex one, and no interpretation yet offered accounts for all its features. The purpose here has been to treat that aspect of it which shows the defensive function of a delusion.

* I find myself in agreement with a recent reviewer of the *Memoirs,* who thinks that whoever reads them "cannot help having doubts about Freud's interpretations of Schreber's experiences."

7. what makes
a delusion?

Delusions or "false believings" are of high importance, since they are found in a number of different kinds of mental illness. Delusions are also important for the striking evidence they provide of the close relation between normal and abnormal behavior.

It hardly need be said that false beliefs are not confined to the mentally disordered. Surely no one is entirely free of them, and it is certain that vast numbers of people live much of their lives believing things that are not true.

It is not, in fact, easy to make a clear distinction between normal delusions and abnormal ones. A popular way of illustrating this is the citing of cases among the great innovators of history who were regarded by their contemporaries as truly deluded, and who turned out, finally, to be right after all.

To be in error in some of one's views is so nearly universal —and human—that it is not hard to find apparent flaws in definitions of delusions which try to make a sharp line between those of healthy and those of disordered people. An intelligent schizophrenic once suggested to me that there might be as many people who believed in astrology as there were patients who believed they had persecutors, that both beliefs were supposed to be false, "yet these folks who believe in astrology are running around loose and *we're* locked up."

In general it may be said that a delusion is likely to be of the abnormal kind when: (1) it has developed by a process of solitary thought, that is, with little or no communication with others regarding its subject; (2) it persists despite frequent encounters with contradictory evidence; (3) there is evidence that the false belief satisfies a need or protects from anxiety; (4) attempts by others to undermine it are met with signs of evasiveness, resistance or considerable emotional warmth.

Many cases suggest that delusions and hallucinations serve the same purpose, or are simply two different methods of defense. We may recall the case of Florrie, who was accused by "voices" of immoral behavior after she had forced from her mind the guilt complex from which she had suffered. The voices represented the change of a self-judgment into a judgment from the world outside. Florrie, instead of being "persecuted" by her conscience, became seemingly persecuted by her neighbors, her office associates and others. By this alteration, she suffered less distress than she would have if she had faced her guilt directly.

Delusions may show the same formula. A recent writer cites the case of a man of 32, who is described as a shy, aloof, timid personality. As a child he felt unjustly accused by his parents. This feeling changed in later years to one of self-accusation, suggesting that the man came finally to accept the judgment of his parents upon him. The feeling of guilt persisted. During a period of mental illness the guilt and self-hatred disappeared, we are told, but he now began to believe that government agents were in pursuit, with unjust accusations against him. One meaning of the paranoid symptom is thus clearly demonstrated. Mental hospital workers would recognize here a familiar delusion, often called the "FBI symptom," because of its marked frequency.

Of this case it is observed that: "The person does not accept self-condemnation any longer as part of the self; condemnation now comes from the persecutors. He does not hate himself anymore; somebody else hates him." [1]

The delusional persecutors thus really represent the parents, who were the original accusers. This leaves the question of the meaning of the substitution. Why are the parents replaced by the FBI, or, as in other cases, the "secret police" or some other organization? Here again, it appears that for a dependent person, with a strong need to feel secure in the affection and regard of his parents, it is painfully distressing to feel that these important people make accusations that imply rejection. The guilt feelings therefore attach themselves to any other person, or to an agency connected with charge-making or investigation. This provides an object for the guilt to focus upon, but being no more than a kind of proxy for the original (parents), it is less threatening and arouses less anxiety.*

the sense of reality

In the case of Schreber a question was encountered that was touched on before: how, unless all ability to reason has been lost, can the mind accept ideas so far from the truth? A common phrase used in the description of the mentally disordered is that they have lost touch with reality.

This may refer to the quality of the false beliefs encountered. There are those that, though false, are fairly plausible. Thus, there was nothing unlikely in Marcella's idea that her neighbors did not care for her personality and so did things to annoy her.

Similarly, there was nothing improbable in Florrie's notion that her love affair had become public knowledge and that people were talking about it, and about her. There might even be those who would find little to question in Marcella's complaint that the noisy truck drivers were a part of the campaign to force her to move away from the neighborhood, or in the panic-stricken interpretations of the man who had offended the "gangsters."

The case records of delusion go far beyond this point, however. Often one seems to be truly "out of bounds," and forced to

---

* The tendency of the thought processes in mental illness to resemble those of dreaming, in which images are so often "selected" to express an emotional state, has been noted. Thoughts of such an organization as the FBI offer an ideal symbol to express a mood of guilt, just as threatening imagery may express anxiety, or sexual imagery an erotic state.

conclude that no normal mind could possibly entertain such beliefs. They suggest a major derangement of the thought processes.

As an example, the patient may be cited who told me that she believed that some of her intimate personal affairs had become publicly known by way of her home television set. It developed that she supposed that television operated in "both directions." She thought that people at the telecasting stations could, if they wished, see into the homes of the viewers by the same means that the latter could see events in the studio.

Must this be called a delusion in the sense in which the term has been used here? It seems a safe surmise that the average housewife knows little or nothing of the technical side of the transmission of images by television. She knows little that would oppose the idea that viewing may work in both directions. Yet it is probably safe to say that the average person would reject this idea with no great hesitation, and that, while he might be unable to give the sources of his information, he would say that he knew enough about television, nevertheless, to feel fairly sure of his opinion.

Such judgments seem to come from a certain kind of knowledge of what is or is not possible or probable. It is sometimes called a "feeling" for what is true, or likely to be true. Such knowledge may be hard to trace, and yet be fairly reliable. It is a residue of many incidental bits of fact which, while quite unordered in the gathering, yet have a certain over-all order and meaning, since they make possible judgments which have considerable certainty. For example, a person may acquire, through experience, a "knowledge of the ways of men" which, however random in sources, yet gives undeniable skills in practice. This is the sort of knowledge which would enable one, for example, to at once reject as fanciful the delusion of the gangster victim earlier mentioned, whose knowledge of such "ways" was apparently weak enough to permit the belief that revenge for a small offense could survive twelve years, and prompt great labors on the part of his enemies.

It seems safe to assume that the capacity to pick up knowledge of this kind varies from person to person. There will be those who, with equal opportunity to acquire such a sense of reality in certain areas, will have learned very little. Among these we will find some who exhibit a puzzling gullibility in certain directions, and who, though intelligent enough generally, are surprisingly uncritical in some regions of everyday thinking. ("He's an excellent engineer, but in business matters he'll believe anything he is told.") Among these, too, might be found a few, or more than a few, of the mental patients whose delusional formations are striking because they run so directly counter to what is assumed to be common knowledge—thus, the patient who believes that others influence his thoughts, or steal them, or that his enemies have wired his bed to electrocute him, or have arranged to pump gas into his room.

Is this the whole story, and does a weak "sense of reality," whether through lack of opportunity or lack of capacity, tell us why schizophrenics (along with many others), so often believe things that are not true?

the logic-proof box

A major value of such a case as that of Schreber's is the evidence it provides that delusions may develop in people whose mental stature makes it highly unlikely that their grasp of reality is weak. Schreber was a man of broad culture, who had read extensively in the science of his day. He can hardly be compared with patients whose ideas about physical processes develop within a setting of small knowledge of the laws of natural phenomena.

In discussion of the Schreber case the sharpness of the conflict that led to his disorder was stressed. The intensity of the war between morals and sexuality was about as painful as it could well be. It was a situation, perhaps, in which a person might be expected "to believe *anything* rather than *that*." Whatever truth lies in the proposition that, other things being equal, how far a delusion departs from fact depends on the strength of the need it serves, seems well illustrated here.

The question remains, however, how Schreber was able to support his belief about a personal transformation in the face of his undoubted scientific culture and grasp of natural realities, and —some would say—of elementary common sense. It is true that during the early period of his illness he was mentally clouded and confused, and probably too disorganized for any attempt at a logical ordering of experience. The question applies rather to the period when, having regained his coherence and his contact with the world, he continued to express his ideas about a change of sex.

It is hardly necessary to observe that if nothing more were necessary to abolish delusional beliefs than the showing of a proof of their clash with facts, the recovery from this exceedingly common disorder should be rapid and complete. Since they are, instead, notoriously difficult to treat, a clue may be found in the characteristic behavior of such patients when confronted with data that clearly contradict their conviction.

It is suggested in the striking difference between the patient's reaction, when confronted in this way, and his reaction to other topics. It is like running into a wall. He ceases, in a sense, to be a reasonable person. More accurately, he seems either unwilling or unable to *make contact* with the point we are trying to make. The mystery of how the strange ideas are maintained before the contradictory facts vanishes when it is seen that the two are never really allowed to fairly meet. It is as if an actual separation or splitting has taken place in the mind. In this way the delusion is altogether safe from "attack" by information that might jar or destroy it.

Bernard Hart, in his little classic, *The Psychology of Insanity*, has described this phenomenon in a way that can hardly be improved:

> Thus, if a patient believes that he is the king, it is use-
> less to prove conclusively to him that his contention is
> wrong; he remains serenely unaffected. He is, perhaps, well

acquainted with the past history of himself and his family, but it never occurs to him that the facts contained therein are incompatible with the belief that he is the son of George III. He may assure us that he is omnipotent and capable of creating a new universe, and yet the next moment he may ask plaintively to be allowed to leave the asylum, or beg for a small quantity of tobacco. The patient believes that he is the king, and he is also aware of facts which totally contradict that belief; but although both these things exist together in his mind, they are not allowed to come into contact, and each is impervious to the significance of the other. They pursue their course in logic-tight compartments, as it were, separated by barriers through which no connecting thought or reasoning is permitted to pass. Similarly, the patient's belief is unaffected by our scientific demonstration of its impossibility. He understands perfectly each point of our reasoning, but its significance is not allowed to penetrate the compartment which contains his delusion; it glides off as water glides off a duck's back.[2]

self protective

In defending his delusion against the onslaughts of logic the schizophrenic becomes characteristically evasive. He fogs the issue, he filibusters, he follows a zig-zag course before the pursuer. This elusiveness may be understood in part by way of a kind of experience familiar to all of us.

Suppose a topic of conversation arouses strongly uncomfortable feelings. It may be something humiliating, or frightening, or something that causes unpleasant feelings of anger or guilt. Suppose also that someone begins to put questions which threaten to penetrate into this blocked-off region of painful feelings. The natural reaction will be to set going a variety of avoidance maneuvers. Your "answers" become general instead of specific; you become indirect; in response to one question you offer an answer to another, safer one. You go off on tangents; you try to change the subject, or you avoid the threateningly personal direction of the trend by turning it toward the other person and seeking to center it closer to *his* concerns, his interests, problems, etc. The effect of all this, of course—if it is successful—will be to defeat the questioner's efforts to obtain information. His questions are disposed of, rather than answered.

It is often very clear that the schizophrenic is, in a comparable way, maneuvering to guard sensitive areas from a verbal attack. Here, too, the answers suggest a more extreme degree of the same kind of defense, as if the probing has stirred up a subterranean panic. The talk becomes confused and makes little sense, yet still suggests a flight from danger into irrelevancies. The patient is trying to escape, not so much from the questioner as from himself, or from a part of himself. It may be a part that he has buried and cannot face. But it may also be reality itself, whose threatening contacts with a precious delusion he is desperately fending off.

Hart offers an excellent illustration of the way in which such defensive avoidance can lead to apparent irrationalities:

> The patient does not answer our questions but replies with some totally irrelevant remarks, which are often grotesquely inappropriate, and give to his conversation a characteristic aspect of meaningless incoherence. Thus one patient, in whose life a lady of the name of Green had played a very prominent part, replied to the question "Do you know a Miss Green?" with, "Green, that's green, that's blue, would you say that water is blue?" Occasionally the patient dissects the question into its constituent words or syllables, furnishing a string of irrelevant associations to each, and thereby avoiding any direct answer to the question as a whole. Often it can be shown that a patient converses normally except when a question which stimulates the hidden complex is given; his replies then exhibit the peculiar incoherence just described.

Another form assumed by these self-protective reactions is an actual momentary impairment or paralysis of the ability to grasp what is said. Thus, a highly intelligent patient once told the writer: "There are times, when we're discussing certain things, that there is a kind of gap in my understanding. It's like I get confused and can't seem to follow what you are saying." It developed that the "certain things" referred to were grounds advanced against certain features of the patient's delusional system. It was at points at which the evidence was especially clear, it seemed, that the patient's comprehension faltered or failed. This is reminiscent of what one occasionally hears during an argument when one of the participants claims that he does not "follow" the other, which may evoke the reply, "I don't think you *want* to understand."

To sum up, it may be said that foremost among the factors that help in the understanding of delusions is the intensity of the underlying need. This intensity is itself in part a product of the structure of the personality within which the conflict develops. A person with a sexual disposition like Schreber's but with a different character formation, and therefore with a different attitude toward sex, might have managed an adjustment without any great stress. It should also be added that the moral culture of the age and the society in which he lived would have a vital bearing on any such conflict by way of its influence on character itself.

Understanding of the content of delusions may be further aided by considering the limitations of the patient's knowledge, by the degree of development of his sense of reality, and finally, by the logic-tight separation of the beliefs so precious to his pride, or so essential as a bulwark against anxiety, from anything that might shake, weaken or destroy them.

personality and delusion

If it is true that delusions express a person's anxieties, or defend against them, or serve certain needs that have been denied, it follows that his delusions, when and if he develops any, will tend to be an expression of his individuality. They will show the kind of person he is, what his fears, frustrations and conflicts have been. Illustratively, it is as if we might say to the patient, "Tell me your delusions and I will tell you what you are." If they tend to exalt him to an importance beyond his actual role, one may surmise that he has been discontented with his status, and that he has fantasied a greater one. If he is convinced, without discoverable grounds, that condemnatory accusations are circulating about him, the deduction is fairly reliable that he has been suffering from some sort of moral conflict.

Among the several factors that favor the development of delusions, as earlier indicated, is the accuracy of a person's information in the region of his delusional thinking. Such knowledge must surely vary greatly with differences in opportunity to acquire it, and with differences in capacity to acquire it. Once acquired, however, its operation may be affected in a variety of ways. Anything that disturbs or impairs the normal activity of the brain may render a person more susceptible to psychological disorder. He will be more likely to err in his recollections, his judgments and his perceptions of situations. He may suffer reduced ability to keep his attention fixed, to keep track of his whereabouts, or to correctly identify the people about him. He may, most importantly, suffer a reduction in ability to "keep in touch" with reality, and thus to *think with accuracy*. From this it follows that, among other possibilities, he will be more likely to become delusional.

Phenomena of this kind are commonly observed under the influence of fatigue, of alcohol, of fever or in consequence of brain disease or accidental injury. In intoxication, as is well known, what might literally be called a temporary change of personality is occasionally observed. Transitory delusions may appear in the form of misinterpretations. A person regarded as normally of an easy social disposition may decide that he has been treated with disrespect; he becomes offended, and perhaps angry. Or, if he can find listeners, an ordinarily modest person may become boastful, and apparently manage to *believe* with sincerity, for a while, that he is a considerably more important or more capable person than the facts would warrant.

It is common, in such cases, to attribute the behavior directly to the alcohol, that is, to see the non-typical or abnormal behavior as a consequence of the abnormal chemical condition. "He's not really like that," one remarks. "It's just that liquor happens to affect him that way."

Studies of what alcohol and other toxic agents do to behavior show, however, that the effects are not to be understood solely in terms of the action of alcohol on nervous tissue. They may also be seen as reflections of internal stresses and conflicts. Behavior changes that appear under such conditions may be viewed as more importantly related to the make-up of the personality than to the direct physical effects of the toxic substances. Delusions that develop in this way tend to reflect the *individuality* of the person concerned.

The excessive use of bromides, for example, gives rise in certain persons to apparently authentic schizophrenic states. Hallucinations occur; persecutory and self-referring delusions are abundant. It was found in one study that these symptoms tend to appear in persons whose normal personalities bear certain resemblances to schizophrenic behavior. In these patients, moreover, the delusional formations exhibited a highly personal stamp. The hallucinations revealed the innermost secrets and preoccupations of the patient's past. The illness, though chemically induced, thus reflected the basic personality. Other patients, also exhibiting the mental effects of bromide intoxication, failed to show comparable symptoms.

Even in brain disease, it has been pointed out, the behavior changes tend to correspond with personal individuality, rather than with the specific damage to the nervous system. It has, in fact, been suggested that if a person were well enough known, the form of the disorder that would result from brain disease could be fairly well predicted in advance. Thus, in one case a patient exhibited a fairly typical persecutory delusion and was then found to be suffering from an organic brain disease (syphilitic). It was reported of the patient that he had always been an "insecure, suspicious" person, and that the delusional behavior was altogether in harmony with his personality structure. In some instances the disorder brought on by brain disease reappeared in identical form long after recovery from the disease, in response to emotional stresses.

Such reactions may be compared with any other in which one and the same situation or stimulus evokes different reactions in different people. They can be compared, for example, with the perception of inkblots in a popular personality test, in which what the blots appear to represent varies greatly from one person to another. Here what is "seen" is often a reflection of the emotional disposition, of experiences, of needs and conflicts of needs.

Such findings, in general, add strength to the view that the symptoms of disorder become *meaningful* primarily through psychological factors even when physical disturbances unquestionably play a part. To the factors previously enumerated as central to the formation of delusions there may be added the weakening of reality contact by way of disease, injury or toxic agents.

false beliefs may not be "delusions"

In judging human beliefs from the standpoint of their departure from reality, it is of high importance to consider the setting in which they have developed. It may be found that the character of a belief may be greatly altered in complexion when this setting is considered.

Behavior was reported of the French novelist, Huysmans, for example, that on the surface would be strongly suggestive of a schizophrenic. At one period of his life he feared invisible and malignant influences; he experienced strange bodily sensations which he attributed to the hatred of his enemies; he felt buffeted, at times, by unseen blows. He obtained some paste that had been "blessed in all sorts of ways," supposedly potent for warding off evil spirits. This he would burn, while reciting "conjurations" intended to paralyze the power of his enemies. These rituals he practiced before retiring.[3]

A psychiatrist, hearing of such bizarre actions by a highly intelligent man, might at once suspect a mental abnormality. But this was the Paris of the late 1800s, in which, in certain social circles, occultism, spiritualism and "satanism" were much in vogue. Huysmans was closely associated with others of like interest. He was a serious and critical student of the supernatural, attended seances, sought experimental data and documented accounts of occult phenomena. One of his novels "tells of the occultist and spiritualist revival which took place in France in the eighties, and reflects the state of mind of a generation which . . . sought comfort in spiritualism, theosophy and even satanism . . ."

His interest in the bizarre and the abnormal, his fascination with things weird and diabolical, were in part, it appears, an attempt to escape from what he repeatedly experienced as the boredom and drabness of life. If he became himself infected by some of the beliefs he examined, he was not alone in this. These beliefs were shared by many; Huysmans was no deviant. If he did attend a "Black Mass," as was reported, the significant thing is that there were such masses to attend, and that the paste he used to drive off evil influence was supplied by others, who also believed in its powers, and in the evils from which it gave protection.

What a person believes is thus not always a reliable mark of delusional thinking. Thus, in several mid-Southern states individuals have been admitted to mental hospitals with manifest delusional systems, including the belief that they could handle live rattlesnakes and drink quantities of poison with impunity—only for it to be discovered later that these "delusions" are standard beliefs of a snake-handling cult, dogmas for which they could cite scriptural support.

It is not enough to compare the patient's ideas, however carefully, with what is considered normal thinking in the social group to which the psychiatrist belongs. These ideas must be compared, as well, with the standards of normality of the group to which the *patient* belongs, if this group differs from that of the psychiatrist. By the same logic, entire groups of people might

very well be considered schizophrenic if their beliefs deviate too
far from what is considered normal in the culture of the psychiatrist.* Further examples of beliefs "normal" to large groups of
people, which closely resemble those of a disordered mind, will
be illustrated in a later chapter. As La Barre says, man is unique
among animals in his ability "to know things that are not so." [5]

---

* H. G. Wells remarked that some of the inscriptions found on ancient
Mayan sculptures resemble drawings made by patients in European mental
hospitals, and that they appear to represent a mentality different in kind,
and to a Western European, not rational at all. Whether the suggested
resemblance is valid or not, the observation illustrates the idea that to one
society another may seem as deviant as some of its own members who are
classed as ill.[4]

8. the inside story

What sort of experience, if any, does a normal person have or might he have which gives a glimpse of how it feels to be schizophrenic? Perhaps the feelings a normal person experiences just after awakening from a very vivid dream that has been bizarre or frightening show some similarity. Though one is fully conscious, the strange mood of the dream is still active, coloring everything. You are awake, but still half dreaming. You feel disorganized, bewildered, unsure of yourself. The familiar, secure sense of self has been shattered. The reality of the dream is still as great, perhaps greater, than the reality of your surroundings. For a few seconds the world has "gone queer." Here, briefly, a normal person may touch upon one of the phases of the mental state of the schizophrenic.

Another example is the experience of a healthy person overwhelmed by a personal crisis in which a looming threat progressively builds anxiety up to a peak of panic. The threat must be a deeply shattering one in which a vital value is at stake. Preoccupation becomes intense; all else is excluded; other persons become unreal, shadowy figures. The sequence of thoughts is broken into incomplete and spasmodic fragments. There is mental clouding and confusion. In this state, desperate or impossible solutions of the problem come to mind and are even accepted, so that for minutes, perhaps even for hours, you may be truly deluded. Later, when calm returns you realize with a shock how disordered your grasp of reality had become. Morale is deeply shaken, and henceforth you find personal meaning in the familiar phrase, temporary derangement.

The resemblance of some of the experiences in mental illness to features of normal dreaming has long been recognized. Again and again, in listening to a patient recount certain experiences, one is struck by this likeness. The kind of thinking that occurs in dreaming and some of the trends of schizophrenic thought, have been seen to be essentially the same. There have been cases in which patients retain, in waking life, delusions formed in dreams. A schizophrenic is reported to have said: "The human dream-life is identical with the sphere of the voices of the insane."

Since most of us dream, the comparison may be helpful. It has often been pointed out, for example, that dreams are true hallucinations. What the dreamer "sees" is as real to him as what the hallucinating patient "hears." The dreamer, too, accepts un-likely happenings; he does not balk at improbable or impossible events any more than the deluded patient balks at improbable or impossible features of his delusions.

Mentally normal dreamers have observed that sometimes the emotions experienced during a dream do not correspond to events. There may be fear, for example, in the absence of any-thing in the dream situation which would give occasion for it, or the dreamer may be in a mood of humor, and feel an impulse to laugh, without relation to events in the dream. Here is a fur-ther resemblance to behavior in schizophrenia, which often dis-plays a striking [inappropriateness of emotional reaction] In the dream, again, there are occasional curious fusions of identity. A person is at once himself and someone else. This is also true of the thought processes of the mentally ill.

Resemblance to both dreaming and to schizophrenic experi-ence has been noted in certain of the novels of Franz Kafka. The narrative often rests on improbable events, and actions which are seemingly lacking in motive. The identity of people is sometimes unstable. Strange, unreal things happen, but are accepted in a quite matter-of-fact way. The mood, the atmosphere, is much of the time distinctively that of a dream, and especially of an anx-ious dream.

Little has been said, so far, of the beginnings of schizo-phrenic illness. Description of our illustrative cases began with the already well-established behavior changes. In some instances these changes appeared gradually over a considerable period of time. In others the changes occurred suddenly.

This sudden beginning has been described in a variety of ways. Although it may be touched off by an event or incident of some sort, the real core of the experience is an *upheaval from within* the personality. This inner upheaval is absorbing. It may make the patient more or less oblivious of events going on about him. The way he perceives these events, so far as he is aware of them, may be distorted by his emotional condition. This condition is most often characterized by feelings of inadequacy, despair or *panic*. The panic may be the climax of a period of increasing anxiety. As in any strongly anxious state, thinking tends to become disorganized.

An important feature of this experience is the impression that, while the upheaval comes from within, it comes from somewhere outside the familiar boundaries of the self. That is, it comes from a part of the self that has been hidden or unconscious. Anyone who has ever found himself, in some novel situation, acting in an impulsive way that causes him later to ask: "What on earth made me do that?" or, "What got into me then?" or "That wasn't like me at all" or similar bewildered phrases, has at least a glimpse, perhaps, of the "feel" of this behavior phenomenon.

The onset of schizophrenia is occasionally announced by an invasion of the mind by unaccountable thoughts and feelings. Often it is fairly clear that the experience is rooted somewhere in the past. A woman patient once had a moment of acute anxiety in my presence, saying that she felt sexually threatened. Though aware that her reaction was irrational, she was unable to account for it. It was finally revealed that she once had been terrified, as a girl, by the sexual advance of an uncle. A male patient who had once undergone severe anxiety in the office in which he had been employed, mistook several other patients in his ward for former office associates. Momentarily, his sense impressions were distorted by an experience out of the distant past, with the result that past and present became mixed together and confused.

One of the best known descriptions of the "inside story" of schizophrenia has been provided by a student of this disorder, Anton Boisen, who was himself a recovered victim. Through first-hand knowledge he was undoubtedly better able to understand and appreciate the meaning of the experience in others. Through study of a large number of cases he came to the conclusion that the core of the illness grows out of a condition of inner disharmony and conflict. There is a profound feeling of personal failure and "an intolerable loss of self-respect." The setting of this experience he found to be *social*, that is, the individual feels that he has failed, and failed in the eyes of his fellows.

The result is a terrifying personal crisis in which thinking becomes disorganized, and in which some remarkable ideas temporarily dominate the mind. There may be a sense that all people, all things, have become involved in the individual's own personal catastrophe. The scale of thinking becomes greatly expanded; the peril seems all-embracing. With the breakdown of the individual's personal world comes the feeling that the rest of the world, too, is breaking down. Great issues are at stake, which may be accompanied by an extraordinary sense of power, of having a mission, of having contact with supernatural forces and beings. Sometimes there is a feeling of being an extraordinary person. All of these sensations and thoughts may be very vivid and quite real to the patient. Ideas of death and rebirth, of having an important destiny, and the feeling that the personal crisis is "cosmic" are found, according to Boisen, in case after case.

In order to understand such seemingly strange experiences the comparison with normal dreaming may again be helpful, along with the idea that some forms of the illness represent a kind of waking dream. Modern dream theory provides the simple principle that while dreams may represent some kind of personal need, or fear or conflict, the *form* in which this is expressed may be greatly altered from the original. The dream story or event *stands for* or symbolizes something else, like an allegory. A familiar example would be the recurrent dream of a college student who had spent four years in the armed service and felt that he was "way behind schedule" in his life plans. Again and again he dreamed that he had to catch an important train, that he had many things to do, was late, and must hurry. The dream was clearly an expression of his impatience with his college work, and the anxious feeling that he must hurry to his destination.

Another student reported a dream following an experience in which he had been in a difficult, awkward and unpleasant social situation from which he was quite unable to extricate himself. In the dream he found himself barefooted, in a field in which a step in any direction meant, because of the peculiarly difficult condition of the ground, a "soggy" or painful or precarious footing.

By this principle it is not difficult to find a meaning in the kind of experience reported by Boisen in one kind of schizophrenic illness. If we begin with his view that this disorder is brought about by an agonizing sense of failure, it is obvious that so sharp a feeling of personal catastrophe could be symbolized by the idea of a *universal* catastrophe, as if to express the collapse of the individual's entire world. Ideas of death and rebirth may be related to the possible wish of one who is frustrated and dissatisfied with himself, to "die" as the person he is, and to become a new personality, closer to his ideal.

The fantasy-like experience of having an important mission may similarly be seen as greatly comforting to a person who feels lost and worthless. For it means to be chosen for an important purpose, to be a part, and an important part, of some great plan. Again, the patient who feels himself to be of heroic proportions is simply trying to escape from his sense of worthlessness and futility.

The apparently weird experiences of the onset of the illness may thus be no more strange than what happens in normal dreaming. Such experiences become more meaningful as—in line with Boisen's thinking—the symbolic expression of a shattering of morale, in which a person "hits bottom" in his valuation of himself, and in some way comprehends that he must either reorganize or perish in spirit. He must break down in order to rebuild. In this sense an acute attack of the illness may in some instances be a turning point in the growth of personality. It may represent, according to Boisen, a kind of spiritual rebirth. It may be a breakthrough which finally leaves behind the attitudes which have been blocking development and crippling a basic life adjustment.

out of the world

The following account of the inside story of acute schizophrenic illness is from a highly intelligent and successful businessman who broke down, in his middle forties, under heavy stresses of overwork and anxiety. Certain features resemble the cases reported by Boisen. At the time of this experience the patient was probably in a stuporous condition, or perhaps in a kind of sleep-walking state. It was set down as told to the writer.

> I had just finished a series of shock treatments. I remember there was a gradual loss of the sense of reality. I had a compulsion to show that I had nothing. I turned my pants' pockets inside out. I felt empty.
>
> Things became less and less real. My surroundings were fading away, I found myself on a different floor in a locked room. I had no recall of being moved. There was a male voice, very distinct, that talked to me. Made remarks about Freudian psychology and about the physical phenomena governing the earth. It told me I was going to see the interior of an atom. I know I lost all consciousness of my surroundings. I was within an atom. I saw the neutrons and electrons, all the parts revolving. Then there was a gap and I awoke in a different room. This was when I had a very wonderful experience. There was a woman, dressed in a kind of robe, white, I think. She was not young or old. She had a strong spiritual quality. She was not beautiful as women are usually considered beautiful. It was a kind of moral beauty.

There was a strong impression that she was timeless, or ageless. She gestured with her hands as she talked.

She talked in the same sort of "cosmic" vein as the voice. She told me the world would not be at peace, that there would be strife and dissension. She said there had been a great mistake in giving the atomic secret to mankind. The gift had been intended to be useful but had been used destructively.

This woman's presence was absolutely no less real than yours is right now. There was also the experience of leaving my body, being off in space. I was completely conscious, but not of my hospital surroundings.

When this woman said "We made a mistake in giving the secret to mankind," that "we" did not include me. Then she said I was to return to the earth. She said something to the effect that I probably would not believe this experience. She said: "I'll give you some proofs." She said I would see her again in the eyes of others. And I did. I mean afterward, several times, there was a certain expression I would see in a person's eyes. The actual expression seemed to change, for an instant. It was like a kind of recognition. It was like looking into their souls.

There was a nurse, I remember; I saw that expression in her eyes. Then there was a volunteer; I saw it in her too. I remember I quoted "We made a big mistake," and then I started to cry. I saw this expression in *your* eyes, too. This look meant one of the proofs. It also meant that I was tuned in, psychologically, to something good and benevolent. It was very reassuring [patient at this point broke into tears, much stirred by his account]. It upsets me to talk about it because it was an experience in which there was perfect love. The woman was a kind of love symbol. There was no carnal element, no physical contact whatever.

The experience was like a kind of reassurance. It seemed to mean that I was to be sent someplace where there was a tough job to do, that is, I had to return to reality. But it was as if to tell me, "We haven't forgotten about you. You aren't alone." I had been feeling very keenly alone, before this happened. Now I had the sense of having perfect tranquility and understanding, and then being told I would have to lose these things again, by "return to earth."

I haven't seen the "look" for some time, now. The woman

resembled no one. She was a complete stranger. She was radiant. The male person (voice only) also expressed a great and deep personal interest in my well-being.

I know this experience must have extended over a period of several days. There were other parts of it, too. I learned afterward about my transfers from room to room during this time. I heard the male voice in one room; later I woke up in another room and it was there I had this experience with the female figure. It was definitely trance-like, but I was conscious of the rooms I was in. I was also conscious of being *in space*. For example, with the woman—I was not in the room with her, but up in space. Occasionally I would wake up, and then I'd recognize a certain room.

[Concerning the immediate background of this experience the patient reports:] This happened during my second hospitalization. The hospital environment had been very upsetting to me. I had been praying to die. I didn't see how a Supreme Being who was supposed to be kind and loving could permit such conditions. I felt bitter against the way I was treated in the hospital, and against my own weaknesses and misfortunes. I talked to one of the doctors, a so-called psychiatrist. He asked me how I was feeling and if I had any enemies. That was about all. He gave me nothing. It was tragic. I think I could have been helped. What I really needed most was to be able to talk with someone. I was in great emotional distress. I needed understanding.

Before this strange experience I remember how completely alone I felt. No one knew what I was going through, least of all the doctors. I needed something no one had ever given me. Not my wife, and certainly not my mother. There was an emotional need. This thing came like an answer. That's why it was so tremendous.

The meaning of the feminine figure is of particular interest, since similar reports have been made by others. Thus, Boisen's central case, during one phase of his illness, had a comparable vision. "He . . . became terror-stricken. He had a vision of a dark woman who seemed to be supernatural. She came and hovered over him and announced that it was time for him to follow her. He became overwhelmed with fear of the unknown. He thought he was going to die. Then he saw things in a new light."

Of the feminine figure the present patient states: "I don't think the idea of a 'mother-figure' would apply here. She was also not a 'goddess.' It seemed to me she was a kind of 'relay-station.'" It is possible that the patient's rejection of the feminine figure as a mother-symbol may be related to strong hostility toward his own mother, and that the figure in his experience *did* stand for at least an idealized mother-image so far as it met his desperate need for contact with a source of reassurance. For at this time he was certainly a wanderer in Boisen's "wilderness of the lost." He needed, in whatever form it might come, what a child seeks in its mother, whether or not he ever found it in her.

The patient further states: "I guess you could say that she was a symbol of love. Or 'Universal Mother' might describe it. The main thing was that I was given to understand that I would not be alone. . . . Both the male and the female figures gave me the feeling that I would have help, and both gave me the thought that what we see as reality is only temporary."

Concerning his brief attack of weeping in recounting the experience, the patient said: "It was the feeling of 'paradise lost' that upset me. Having left something so sublime . . . the grief at the great loss, yet knowing I have to continue on. For several days afterward I had the feeling of being confined, like being encased in something foreign . . . my body. I actually had to become accustomed to being myself again, of coming back from having left."

The patient's "grief at the great loss" tells how strong was the need which was temporarily fulfilled in this experience. One of Storch's patients, after a similar episode, "when she looked back upon her ecstatic state, in which she saw herself and her loved one elevated to heavenly realms, and recognized it as delusional, cried out, sobbing: 'What am I to believe and what not? I don't want any of that to go away—not any part of it!'" [1]

While there was evidence in our patient that a strong feeling of demoralization and abandonment (perhaps symbolized by turning his pockets out) was the immediate background of the experience, his earlier history provides more significant material. The family was an insecure one. The patient recalls severe physical punishment in childhood ("my arms would be black and blue, many times"), and an incident in which he threatened suicide and his mother jeered that he lacked courage: "I felt that she had a pretty low opinion of me." He felt his brother was favored, was "the fair-haired boy" of the family. The marriage failed; the father left his family ("we felt that by leaving us, he rejected us"). He recalls clearly that he felt unwanted: "I think this feeling of worthlessness started then. I remember planning to join the Navy, and thinking my mother would be glad to get rid of me."

Though highly competent in his profession, the patient worried much about the quality of his work. It required considerable traveling away from home, which led to a rift between him and his wife. Hospitalization did little to alleviate a profound feeling of isolation, as his testimony shows. The hallucinatory experience thus appears as in part a response to profound emotional needs rooted in childhood, and reactivated by the stresses of adult life.

The resemblance of such experiences as this to an extraordinarily vivid dream is evident. The dream quality of certain schizophrenic episodes is apparent in a case reported by Storch, which also shows clearly an important feature of this illness, to be discussed later, namely, that the experience may represent a re-arousal out of the past of an acute anxiety.

A sensitive girl had been violated in childhood by her father. She was employed as a servant. One evening the son of her employer had been very friendly, and apparently she felt that his interest was sexual. During the night she was seized with a strange anxiety which was "like a compulsion from the past." She felt sexually threatened by the son, and fled from the house in terror. During her flight, we are told, "it seemed that in spirit she was still at home," and that she had actually been attacked. When finally she came to herself, she returned home, realizing the dream-like character of the experience and the unreality of

the "seduction." The scene of early sex violation was then recalled, though it was with difficulty that she remembered that
the person had been her father.

In his comment on the case, Storch points out the interweav-
ing of past and present in that an anxiety of childhood rose up to
color and distort a later event; ". . . as the earlier situation and
the present are confused, the real seducer of her infancy and the
imagined seducer of the present lose their character as separate
individuals and become condensed, melted together into a single
image." This feature of the case illustrates a further source of
the phenomenon of mis-identification so often seen among schizophrenics: the falsification of reality by long-lasting aftereffects of
the anxious or shock-like incidents of the remote past.

The anxiety may be of a quite different kind, however, and
expressed in an altogether different way. For example, a great
many of us have suffered the throes of indecision through fear of
making a blunder. We may realize fully that the wisest philosophy is to accept the risk of error as a normal human limitation,
to make our choices as best we can, resolved to accept the consequences. When the mind is filled with anxiety, however, it may
be very difficult to put such a philosophy into practice. When
anxiety of this kind reaches an extreme pitch, in fact, the resulting behavior may become extraordinary.

The inner experience of the mute, motionless patient who
appears deeply preoccupied is not easy to recover, since it is
commonly difficult for him to recall the contents of this state
after coming out of it. In a case reported by Arieti, the condition
of immobility is seen as expressing an extreme anxiety which
makes it increasingly difficult for the patient to act. The impossibility of deciding whether to act or not to act rendered the patient incapable of any movement at all. "More and more he realized that it was difficult for him to act. He did not know what to
do. He did not know where to look, where to turn. . . . The
overwhelming fear of doing the wrong thing, which would either
hurt or disappoint him, seemed to possess him to an increasing

degree. . . . He preferred to be motionless . . . to lie in bed or on a chair for a long time."

The background of this patient's illness showed a direct relationship to the disorder described. His unhappy mother had released upon her son the resentment rooted in her marriage. Among other outlets, she constantly belittled and criticized him. Never could he win her approval of anything he did. "If he turned on the radio, it was the wrong program; if he looked for a job, it was always for the wrong job, etc." As an adult, we are told, his sensitivity to criticism caused him to give up jobs. His lack of confidence became so profound that he ceased to look for work. He stayed at home, "afraid to go out because going out meant making decisions or choices that he felt unable to make. . . . He was increasingly afraid of doing the wrong thing."

It is of some interest to note that in his anxiety and lack of confidence, this patient exhibited a symptom observed in our study of Martha, and probably for the same reason. He sought guidance in "signs." He gave a personalized meaning to chance events. An accidental noise heard at the moment of decision might be taken as a warning not to act. A red traffic light might mean that he should not continue his journey. One is reminded of the people who seek for comparable forms of guidance by a finger placed at random upon a line of the Bible.

from the diary of a schizophrenic girl

Sylvia had not had any dates for a long while. She had not had many opportunities, it was true, but this was rather because of an air of aloofness about her than because of unattractiveness. She appeared uninterested, and men therefore rarely approached her in the office where she worked. She did not seem to need anybody. She seemed absorbed in her work.

But in the evening, in her room in the boardinghouse where she lived alone, she spent many hours thinking, not about her work, but about the people who appeared to mean so little to her during the day. She also thought much about herself, and sometimes she confided these things to her diary. Some of the entries would have surprised anyone who had noticed how self-sufficient she seemed.

"Again that feeling of not belonging . . . neither in the office nor in the world. You want to give to others, but you are too inhibited. You put all your giving into your work, which gives nothing back. That's why you are unhappy. Why don't you give to people, then you will get back in kind? Give and it shall be given you. Be friendly. I don't want to live alone, but that is where I will be if I continue to be aloof. Companionship, that is my goal in life. . . . I want love and companionship, kinship, friendship . . . I carefully preserve myself as the withdrawn type, but I want someone to be with me at the same time."

Sylvia's timidity, and her consequent solitary existence, led to much daydreaming. Although indulgence in wish-fulfilling fantasies gave many hours of enjoyment and greatly relieved her loneliness, she was too intelligent not to realize that it was unhealthy to spend so much time in this way. Diary entries show that she occasionally scolded herself for it: "I am tired of saying 'I can't' and living in an unreal world. . . . You have been rationalizing all this time. . . . You make up a world to believe in instead of acknowledging the real world. . . . Preferring dreams to reality, that's the whole story." She became listless, and spent much time making observations on herself and others. Commenting on this period, she observed: "Life didn't seem to matter a lot. I mean, I was overwhelmed with ideas. Thinking about life was more interesting than life itself."

Sylvia felt interested in certain girls in her office. It seemed to her that these girls appeared slightly confused in her presence, that they blushed or paled slightly when they saw her. From this she inferred that they were attracted to her. She once phoned one of these "smitten" girls and asked if she would like to spend the night together. In explaining her motive, Sylvia said: "She had to be made to realize what it was she wanted of me. When I called her up all I wanted was for her to realize that this thing was abnormal and must stop. I thought she did not know her impulses were homosexual, or rather that she could not face them. I wanted her to know where her impulses would lead, and that she was playing with fire. It worked, and she refused, and was walking around blushing for several days."

This is an excellent example of the kind of thinking called rationalization. Sylvia herself made the advance, but managed to persuade herself that her sole motive was to make the girl aware it was *she* who was attracted to Sylvia. It was a neat way of shifting, or reversing the fact that she herself was the attracted one.

The social shyness of the schizophrenic is well illustrated in Sylvia's behavior. Thus, in this instance, an outright advance would have been impossible for her. Only by disguising her motive was she able to be so daring. Typically, she was more roundabout in her approaches. One Christmas the girls exchanged gifts. Sylvia gave one girl a book dealing with the Kinsey report. This she did because: "I thought that since it would get around to everyone that I had given Mary the Kinsey book it would get to Lila too, and she would realize that she might have Lesbian qualities." Lila was the goal of this maneuver. Sylvia commented, "Yes, I realize it was indirect, but it was about as direct as I can be. I'm pretty cautious in such matters."

Sylvia is tall, rather slender, with black hair and greyish eyes. While her features are good, there is a slightly masculine quality about them. During experiences such as those reported above, she feels that she may be homosexual. She has had rather strongly negative feelings toward men. Some of her remarks tell us clearly, however, what these feelings come from.

"My mother and father were very unhappily married. My father got drunk pretty regularly and was brutal to my mother. He was critical of us, and demanding. I think my feeling of distrust or aversion toward men began with my father. We were belittled so much, I didn't think any man would want me. . . . He was never really affectionate. He was a small-minded, envious man who belittled everything. . . . I hated Pa for a long time.

Now I feel sorry for him because I see he could not do anything different; because he copied his forebears and their treatment of him."

Sylvia's attitude toward sex was colored by certain early impressions in which the image of her father was again central. "Maybe it was because of my father. I remember my mother would be alseep after working all night. My father would wake her up with his face flushed and with an angry expectant look. He looked ugly and selfish. I've seen him grimace and leer when he talked about marriage."

Sylvia's mistrust of men, with its source in the family, was strengthened by later events. In some sex relationships she had felt degraded because she thought she had been "used" rather than loved. There appeared to be, on the whole, no reason to doubt that her basic attitude toward men and toward sex was potentially a healthy one, and that it had been spoiled by some unfortunate experiences.

During the early period of her hospitalization the line that divides the real from the unreal for most of us became confused. She developed a delusion in which her fantasy life was clearly evident. Fantasy, in other words, had become a part of reality. She had once been attracted to a male office associate. She spoke little to him, had never dated him, did not really *know* him at all, but thought about him often. At the hospital she expressed belief that he had become seriously interested in her, that he was, in fact, making some plans for her future. In newspaper captions and on radio programs she found statements that seemed to have a personal reference. In some way, she felt, her "lover" was behind these things. "Sometimes I think he is trying to reach me this way. I think he is trying to change my personality to be more acceptable to him. I feel that I am immature."

Some of the communications came in code-like form. For example, she felt that the song "Mule Train" had a personal meaning, linked with her lover. "Train" was to be taken in the sense of "teach." "A mule is obstinate, which I felt I had been.

So I thought it meant he wanted to reeducate a stubborn person."

Sylvia had moments of insight: "If I thought it wasn't really true—I mean, that he really wasn't behind these things, it would be a blow."

The last comment reflects plainly the emotional need from which delusions may grow. It also hints of an important reason why such delusions are difficult to remove: the patient does not *want* to lose them. To deprive Sylvia of hers would mean to increase her loneliness, and to confirm her feeling of rejection.

the search for identity

An important part of the development of personality is the growth of the *idea of the self*. This idea includes an answer to such questions as: What *am I* in the eyes of others? How do they see me, or rate me? Do they accept me? What is my status and role?

Part of the answer comes to us through learning what we can or cannot achieve. It comes through successes and failures in social activities. A very vital part of it comes to us, however, through experiences in which others show us how we appear to them. Some individuals owing to various unfortunate circumstances may fail to develop an adequate or accurate "idea of self."

A girl, born into an unstable, and finally a broken, family, spent many years of her growth period in foster homes. Her unruly behavior caused her to pass through a considerable number of such homes, often remaining for only a few months. Being sensitive, she often noticed that her foster parents treated her differently than they treated their own children. Rarely was she able to feel that she fully belonged in the family circle, and rarely was she able to develop any clear idea of where she stood, how she was regarded as an individual. The relationships were too brief, too changeable, and the experiences were contradictory or inconsistent.

Her fumbling and uncertain efforts to find her place in society is evident in the following account of what she regarded, at the age of 24, as the basic question confronting her in face-to-face relationships with others.

I just can't seem to find my place in relation to other people. I keep wondering what people think of me. When they look at me I feel they think I'm queer or odd. I seldom feel equal to others. I feel that people always expect less of me than they do of others.

Other people seem to step in and out of social relationships so easily. I seem to be always standing off to the side, wondering about doing or saying the wrong thing. I always feel I must prove myself. I spend most of my time with people trying to keep up their faith in me.

I realize that this has gone to extremes. My very existence seems to depend on whether people reject or accept me. I keep analyzing the way they act toward me. I try to keep myself in a position so whether they accept or reject me I won't be upset. I mean I keep myself sort of ready to change according to the way they treat me. Sort of plastic. But I don't want to be just a piece of clay, molded by the action of others. I want to be a person, an individual.

Other people take friendliness and friendship for granted, but for me it's a kind of prize to be won.

There's a lot of make-believe in people. They show it in their faces. They don't have sincerity. I watch for the slightest defect in sincerity. I'm very sensitive to people.

This is all *very* important to me. It's my very breath.

I never seem to feel sure of my position in relation to others, but usually I'm more sure of their being negative toward me than of anything else. It's the way people *look* at me. If they really are friendly, why do I get the impression they are rejecting me? You say this probably isn't true. How can I see it that way and yet convince myself that it *isn't* rejection? How can I seem to see what *isn't* so clearly? How can you tell? What's real and what isn't real?

I'm not really certain of what I am. I mean, I take other people's treatment to show me what I am, since I'm not sure myself.

But people seem to be so continually in a state of change. It's hard to know what you are, this way.

I'm unable to act because of constant doubt and misgivings.

Thinking about things like this, it's the only security I've got. Then, at least, I'm real to myself. This at least is what I am.

another famous schizophrenic

The great Swedish dramatist, August Strindberg, passed through a schizophrenic illness of which he left a vivid account in his autobiographical writings. During his middle forties, living alone in Paris, experimenting with alchemy, and often nearly destitute, he experienced a number of the classical features of the disorder.

The "plan delusion," as seen in the case of Martha, is evident in much of Strindberg's story. The thought that Providence was designing events for him is expressed again and again. Thus: "The existence of the invisible Hand, which guides me over rough paths, has become a certainty to me, I no longer feel solitary . . ."

He repeatedly perceived events and objects as having a personal meaning:

> One morning I awoke with the idea of making a trip into the country. . . . I take the train for Meudon. I go into the village itself, which I visit for the first time, traverse the main street, and turn to the right into a narrow alley confined by walls on both sides. Twenty steps before me I see half-buried in the ground the figure of a Roman Knight in grey iron armour. It looks very well moulded, but, as I approach, I see that it is only rough metal-smelting. . . . The knight looks towards the wall, and following the direction of his gaze I notice something written on the mortar with a piece of coal. It looks like the letters F and S interlaced, which are the initials of my wife's name. She loves me still! The next moment I see, as by a flash, that it is the chemical symbol for ferrum (iron) and sulphur, and the secret of gold lies revealed before my gaze. . . . I return to Paris with the lively

impression of having experienced something bordering on the marvellous.[2]

He is about to enter a house, but sees a child on the threshold with a playing card in its hand. The card is a spade. He concludes that an "evil game" is being played within, and leaves. Again, he sees upon the ground some dry twigs which form two letters of the name of an enemy whom he fears. "He *was*, then, persecuting me, and the powers wished to guard me against the danger." He is subjected to a variety of annoyances in public places, behind which he sees, sometimes "providence," sometimes the "Evil One." A weather cock "seems to me to flap its wings as though it wished to fly northward." From this impression he concludes that fate ordains his departure from Paris. He often seeks signs, opening the Bible or other books at random. Nothing is too trivial to have meaning. There are no accidents. The name of a street he is passing through, even the movements of an insect on his writing desk, have a personal message for him.

At times he feels guided and protected by invisible forces: "The powers seem to be gracious to me, and to have arranged the sufferings they have ordained for my improvement." There are times, however, when the behavior of his friends is altered, when concealed hostility is evident in "looks and innuendoes," and there are periods when he lives in acute anxiety of the machinations of enemy forces, focusing upon the vengefulness of a man whom he has offended. He fears that poison gas is being discharged into his room, and that an electrical machine is being used against him.

In the evening I dare not remain sitting at my table for fear of a new attack, and lie on the bed without venturing to go to sleep. The night comes and my lamp is lit. Then I see outside, on the wall opposite to my window, the shadow of a human shape, whether a man or a woman, I cannot say, but it seems to be a woman. When I stand up, to ascertain which it is, the blind is noisily pulled down; then I hear the Unknown enter the room, which is near my bed, and all is silent.

For three hours I lie awake with open eyes to which sleep refuses to come; then a feeling of uneasiness takes possession of me; I am exposed to an electric current which passes to and fro between the two adjoining rooms. The nervous tension increases, and, in spite of my resistance, I cannot remain in bed, so strong is my conviction: "They are murdering me; I will not let myself be murdered." I go out in order to seek the attendant in his box at the end of the corridor, but alas; he is not there. They have got him to go away; he is a silent accomplice, and I am betrayed! [3]

Again and again, in different lodgings, the idea of "electrical persecutions" obsesses him, and he spends whole nights in panic as "discharges" and "fluids" threaten and oppress him. He is driven from one place to another for refuge. He is suspicious, cannot trust even a doctor, and in the home of the doctor with whom he takes a room, he suspects that the brass ornaments on his bed may be "conductors," its copper springs "induction coils," and a roll of wire netting in the room above, an "accumulator." He finds other evidence to support the belief that the doctor is one of his persecutors, although "he only plays the role assigned to him." (The last assumption reflects Strindberg's idea that the action of certain people toward him is an expression, not of their own initiative, but of the influence of "The Powers.") On another occasion he is driven from his bed at night, and from his room, by an electric current, which "streams through the wall on my bed, seeks my breast, and under it, my heart." These emotions are usually experienced at night; they are accompanied by a tightness of the chest and sensations of suffocation and palpitation.

The latter symptoms are clearly suggestive of an attack of anxiety. The roots of Strindberg's anxiety were deep. He had been a fear-ridden child. "He seemed to have been born frightened, and lived in continual fear of life and of men." He feared, he says, "the darkness and blows . . . feared to fall . . . to go in the streets. . . . Feared the fists of his brothers, the roughness of the servant-girl . . . the rod of his mother . . . his father's cane. . . . feared the landlord's deputy, when he played in the courtyard with the dust-bin . . . feared the landlord . . ." He feared other children, feared water, feared night noises. Like his brother and sister, he feared his father. "When the cry 'Father is coming!' was heard, all the children ran and hid themselves, or rushed to the nursery to be combed and washed. At the table there was deathly silence . . ."

He was very sensitive and cried easily. "He wept so often that he received a special nickname for doing so. He felt the least remark keenly, and was in perpetual anxiety lest he do something wrong." One brother was the father's favorite, another the mother's; Strindberg was no one's favorite. "The child heard only of his duties, nothing of his rights. Everyone else's wishes carried weight; his were suppressed. He could begin nothing without doing wrong, go nowhere without being in the way, utter no word without disturbing someone. At last he did not dare to move."

Discipline was strict, disobedience severely punished. When the child once protested innocence of an offense, he was deemed guilty nonetheless, and flogged till he "confessed." The mother, tired from bearing a large family, was sometimes unjust and violent. The boy could confide in no one, felt surrounded by enemies. Obedient and conscientious though he was, resistance was growing; at times something "hard and cold" rose within him.

From the mother the children received "food and comfort . . . therefore they loved her." To Strindberg she became a glorified symbol of all that he needed most. The "feeling of loneliness and longing after his mother followed him all through his life. Had he come perhaps too early and incomplete into the world? What held him so closely bound to his mother?"

It is clear that Strindberg felt oppressed, unloved and rejected within his family. He was unfairly treated, he thought, and felt himself an outsider. He repeatedly refers with bitterness to his early life as extremely painful. Yet the ties of family remained strong in him; he felt a close bond of sympathy with his brothers, was quite capable of homesickness. His mother continued to stand as an ideal of protectiveness and warmth. He was also becoming conscious of his extraordinary gifts: conscious that his power was developing. "In all his weakness he sometimes was aware of enormous resources of strength, which made him believe himself capable of anything." Yet he also confesses that he became frightened when he contemplated his own egotism, and felt that he had "sinned through conceit." He was, in fact, later to interpret the terrible experiences of his illness as a retribution.

He experienced significant preliminaries many years before the onset of the illness. He was subjected to unaccountable periods of anxiety which caused him to fear people. There were times when the "terrible helplessness of childhood" returned to him, "the fear of loneliness, of people, of . . . the dark," and vivid details came back out of the past. He says he "had in fact never grown up." Before the breakdown he predicted: "I shall crack either into insanity from agony of conscience, or into suicide." He writes later of the torment of memories, in daylight as well as at night, of "faults, crimes, and follies."

There is ample evidence here of the guilt conflict so often discovered among the sources of the persecution complex. Strindberg speaks of being persecuted by "the consciousness of guilt"; of a "tender conscience, which suffered at every step he took lest it should vex his father or friends . . ." Again, he writes of a "severe struggle with his conscience" regarding a promise made to his father. He describes himself as inclined to self-torment.

His over-sensitiveness to rejection caused him to continually feel spurned, and kept alive the hostility already traceable in childhood. The hostility, in turn, aroused guilt and anxiety. He writes of "the scourge of conscience, which causes me to suspect enemies everywhere; enemies, *i.e.*, those injured by my evil will." Elsewhere he writes: ". . . my conscience smites me every time that I come on the track of a new foe."

Strindberg, like Kafka, endured a persecution complex dating from childhood and grounded in early anxiety and guilt feeling, dogging the emotional life far into the immature adulthood. Both sought to break free of childhood bonds and habits in the struggle toward individuality.

9. the flight

from reason

Many of us, doubtless, have had occasion to remark after a conversation: "I knew what he was saying, but I didn't know what he was talking about. Somehow we were never talking about quite the same thing." With the schizophrenic, this problem is apt to occur to a remarkable degree. As one student puts it, "Everyone who begins to work with schizophrenic persons finds himself involved sooner or later in a very baffling situation. Although both he and the patient seem to be talking about the same thing, they are repeatedly missing each other's points."[1]

The seeming unreasonableness of the patient when evidence is offered against one of his delusions was described in Chapter 7. By many devious turns he takes flight from logic. He escapes into unimportant details, eludes the point behind a cloud of words, and will not be pinned down, no matter how often one repeats the question which probes his emotional conflict, or which touches too closely the sensitive areas of anxiety. He is exhibiting an extreme example of the familiar avoidance behavior that is normally prompted by a painful topic.

One of the commonest features of this kind of thinking is its "scattered" quality. Again and again, the patient seems to lose his sense of direction and wanders into bypaths. It is as if he has become, for some reason, extremely distractible. Sometimes the thought that sets him off on a tangent seems merely distant from the central theme. Sometimes his attention appears to have been derailed by an accidental impression, something seen or heard.

He is diverted by far-fetched associations or by the mere sound of the words or by meanings that do not fit the setting, as when, asked whether something was "weighing heavily on his mind," a patient replied: "Yes, iron is heavy." By taking the idea of *weight* in its physical sense, he had broken sharply away from the theme of the question. A young girl once responded to the word "wood," with the phrase, "that . . . Max would come to life again," and we are told that here "wood" suggested "coffin," and the latter the thought of a dead person, this because of an unhappy love affair.

Obviously, emotional factors may be involved in such curious departures from the expected course of thinking, and sometimes the role of personal conflicts is quite clear. For example, an effeminate boy had been talking quite logically as a member of a group of patients who met for discussions, until one day the topic of homosexuality was introduced. At this point he broke off with a question about a design on the carpet, and for several minutes his comments remained irrelevant. Another patient frequently intruded into the conversation the remark that she was a "little lemon," thus expressing her preoccupation with the thought that she was immature and inadequate ("little") and a coward (lemon colored, or "yellow"). Again, the schizophrenic may allow certain associations to alter the course of his thoughts; thus, in naming the members of his family, a patient followed "father" and "son" with "Holy Ghost" and "Holy Virgin."

The general tendency toward scattering has sometimes been treated as a loss of ability to keep essential thoughts gathered together upon the subject, and to screen out what is not related. The schizophrenic "is shooting at the target with a verbal shotgun where he should be sighting along a rifle." [2] While his comments may be within the general region of conversation, they may be so far out of focus as to seem at first impression to be missing the mark altogether.

On the surface, it is true, this does look like an actual loss of ability to keep the mind properly *set*. The evidence suggests, however, that here again the schizophrenic is trying to keep away from the heart of the matter. What he says often appears to be a kind of compromise between coming to the point and leaving it altogether. Behind the seeming haphazardness one glimpses the shadowy outline of a purpose.

Some of the peculiar speech usages appear to be highly individual word habits. The schizophrenic speaks in a very personal idiom. Thus, one patient said he "has *menu* three times a day," rather than "meals" or "food."[3] Another is bothered by the "outward hollerings" of other patients, meaning their noisy outbursts. One says he is "blued-off" when one of his letters is returned to him with a notice penciled on it in blue ("addressee unknown"). Another says, "as a child I was already an apartment," meaning that she was different from others, and thus, in a sense, "apart" from them. Another, referring to his brother's way of agreeing easily with others, says: "There's nothing wrong with Gene, except whoever he's with he flows right along with that person."

These are curious ways of expression, to be sure. While understandable, they are certainly not familiar language. They suggest that some people, while retaining the basic vocabulary of English, have developed some very private modes of speech, a practice not altogether unknown to supposedly normal people. In the schizophrenic, however, this practice may reach a degree that makes him very hard to follow. "The schizophrenic becomes so used to his own language that he is no longer able to tell people what he thinks even when he feels like doing so."[4] Why anyone should develop language habits of this kind, and become so accustomed to them as to have trouble in communicating with others is, of course, a question that must be answered.

Sometimes the disturbed thinking suggests the effect of unusual preoccupation. A person greatly absorbed in his own thoughts may find it difficult to shift gears when an altogether new topic is introduced. His central interest may be so insistent that his response to other subjects may be so colored that whatever he says is a mixture of the old thoughts and the new. Here is another tendency often observed in normal behavior which may reach an extreme degree in mental illness.

As an example of this, a patient of only fair intelligence had been greatly absorbed in fantasies of being a great engineer. When asked to complete the sentence beginning: "My hair is brown because ———," he answers: "Because it is a sort of hydraulic evering. [What does that mean?] It means that it gives you some sort of a *color blindness* because it works through the *roots of the hair* and hydrasee . . . That is a study of the *growth of plants,* a sort of *human* barometer, hydraulic hydroscenic method." [5] The words in italics show the effects of the question upon the patient's usual preoccupations. He has coined some words, apparently to give his remarks as scientific a flavor as possible. The passage illustrates, moreover, the patient's absorption with scientific fantasies—doubtless imagining himself a great engineer—which has caused him to answer a simple question in a high-sounding way. His technical ideas have gotten mixed up with the idea of hair color to produce a confused hodge-podge, but not a meaningless one if we see where its ingredients come from. A patient of this type "constantly interjects into his speech and language words and sentences which have a good deal to do with his own personal problems but nothing to do with the subject at hand." [6]

Another peculiarity of the mental processes of the schizophrenic is commonly called "blocking." Conversation with the patient may end abruptly because he ceases, perhaps in mid-sentence, to speak. He has apparently gone blank. Questioning usually fails to throw much light on the matter; the patient may say only that he does not know why he stopped.

It is generally accepted that blocking means that the course of thought has touched upon a painful complex. The block is, in effect, a mental barrier erected in defense against the arousal of emotion. Thus, it is reported that a young girl, talking freely of her past life, suddenly stopped. Later she recalled, through an indirect approach, that her story had reached the period at which

she met her sweetheart. Another patient, in severe conflict about
her marriage, blocked when the word "divorce" was introduced.
Later she referred to it as a "horrible word." It is clear that many
of the strange features of schizophrenic conversation become
understandable when it is assumed that the patient is taking
flight from a question that is too close to a painful topic
(or "complex"), or because he has developed some highly personal ways of expressing himself.

a method in the madness

There is a kind of delusion that appears in a different setting from those described earlier. One patient announces, for
example, that she is the Virgin Mary. Another proclaims "I am
Switzerland," or "I am Schiller's Bell." Such patients may be able
to offer little bases for their beliefs. They may exhibit a number
of seemingly unconnected delusions without comprehensible
logic. They may also show disturbances in other regions of
thought. Such cases seem to illustrate the old view that mental
illness is simply a disease of the nervous system, and that symptoms mean only that the machinery is out of order and its performance therefore abnormal. Such symptoms may "mean" no
more than the disorganized and haphazard sounds of a defective
motor. In earlier descriptions of delusional people it was stressed
that thinking ability outside the area of the delusion might be
quite unimpaired and that the false belief might serve the purpose of defending against a distressing emotional crisis of some
sort.

It now appears that there are forms of the disorder in which
the thinking processes are more widely affected. If we are to
keep to our original view of the meaning of mental disorder—
and to persist in believing that it *has* a meaning—it must be assumed that in these cases the measures needed to protect against
painful conflict involve the thinking processes in a more extensive way. The needs of defense may reach a point at which

much of what is called normal logic must be sacrificed. What looks on the surface like a breakdown of normal thinking is, instead, a purposive flight from a reality that has become too charged with anxiety to be tolerated. There is evidence, in fact, that what appears as impaired ability to reason correctly is, instead, a *change in the method of reasoning.* The purpose of this change is not only to protect the self, but to satisfy certain other needs as well.

This is to suggest that what is commonly regarded as *disorder* is, rather, *an order of a different kind,* and one very different from the thinking habits of normal people, which is undisturbed by severe emotional stresses. The normal order of human thinking is governed by the requirement of the real world, as well as by individual needs. The strangely altered "order" of schizophrenic thinking is governed much less by the world as it is, and much more by individual needs.

After a thorough study a student recently concluded that one of these altered modes of thinking is a tendency to regard as identical, things which would normally not be so considered. Thus, two different objects or persons, alike in a certain way, will be regarded as altogether *the same* because of this likeness.

Suppose, for example, a young girl with strong religious feeling and a rather glorified ideal of maidenly purity suffers severe conflict because of natural erotic impulses she is unable to overcome. She attempts to deny her erotic nature, but the struggle continues until her thinking becomes confused and disorganized. In the hospital she refers to herself as a saint (she had idealized the famous feminine saints of history) and finally proclaims herself the Virgin Mary. This delusion undoubtedly expresses the most intense longing of her nature. It gratifies not only her ideal of purity, but stands for what to her is the highest possible spiritual achievement.

How could this girl regard herself as the Virgin Mary? The answer we are offered is that when emotional need is great, a kind of logic may come to the rescue which allows conclusions on the basis of certain limited resemblances where normal logic would require much more. It is as if the girl's reasoning were expressed: "Mary was a virgin; I am a virgin; therefore I am Mary." While by normal standards this is an absurd deduction, to say the least, it may be seen as a further example of what may happen to thinking when emotional disturbance becomes overwhelming. It is another, and an extreme, case of "needful believing." It might be said, perhaps, that the patient "needed to identify herself with the Virgin Mary because of the extreme closeness and spiritual kinship she felt for the Virgin Mary." [7] This need was unusually acute probably *because* of the girl's struggle with what she regarded as sinful impulses.

Could it not be said that such deluded reasoning really does mean an actual breakdown of normal thinking, and that the patient has simply taken advantage of this breakdown, so to speak, in order to believe what she wishes to believe? What can be the grounds for regarding such thinking as expressing, instead, a certain kind of logic?

An answer has been offered that we cannot regard this kind of thinking as truly disordered because there are vast numbers of normal people who habitually engage in it. These are the people who are classed as primitive or as "savages" (sometimes more charitably referred to as the "simpler" peoples). Other modes of thinking or reasoning which are very different from those we regard as rational are *normal* to them. Here, too, different things may be identified on the basis of certain similarities.

Primitive people often regard different objects as identical on the basis of the emotional state associated with them. "Star and flower, man and animal, are identified not because they are conceived as exhibiting any material likeness but because they are *felt* as identical." In certain rituals in which a person takes the role of an animal, he is quite literally regarded as *being* the animal. Thus, a case is cited among some North Brazilians who regard themselves as red parrots. There was evidence that these people did not mean merely that they were related to parrots; they asserted that they were actually transformed into parrots, "much as a caterpillar might say it was a butterfly."

It is not uncommon for a primitive man to think he *is* not only himself but an ancestor who lived earlier. This phenomenon of identifying two different persons is characteristic of schizophrenics. Thus, a patient identified herself with her patron saint, St. Theresa. She believed herself to be this saint, even though she was aware that the saint had lived at an earlier time. Another patient regards the ward "doctor" as her father, and the other patients as her sisters. The similarity is that both the doctor and her father are in positions of authority, and that the other patients and herself are in a dependent position, as sisters would be.

Such parallels have been used to support the view that the schizophrenic has reverted to a primitive form of thinking. He has, in a sense, became psychologically primitive. Because of the difficulties he has encountered in getting along with reality at the complex level of civilized living, his mind has gone back, or been driven back, to an earlier and simpler kind of reasoning, a more instinctive kind of logic.

Yet this conclusion does not follow necessarily from the facts. It may be doubted, moreover, that it makes the behavior to which it has been applied more understandable. The fact that schizophrenic disorders occur among primitive peoples has been taken to argue against it. A conclusion which seems equally permissible, and more helpful in understanding this illness, is that the thinking of both schizophrenics and primitives appears to be more closely bound to emotional states and to personal needs.

escape from meanings

It was earlier noted that the schizophrenic may seize upon certain words and take them in a sense other than what was intended, apparently as a means of evading a topic. He may use the mere sound of a word to go off on a tangent. At times he appears to move away from the more general meanings of words, as if to take them only in the simplest way possible. Thus a patient was asked to tell what was meant when a human being was re-

ferred to by the name of an animal, and was given the word
"wolf." He was able to reply only that a wolf was a "greedy
animal."

The same kind of confinement to the simplest or narrowest
meanings may be illustrated when a patient is asked to tell what
a proverb means. Thus, for the proverb: "When the cat's away
the mice will play," one patient could say only that ". . . when
the cat is away, the mice take advantage of the cat." A schizophrenic considered the proverb: "A rolling stone gathers no
moss" to mean quite literally that moss will not grow on a moving stone. His thinking could not, it seemed, rise above the concrete level of meaning.

The meanings of words sometimes seem confined to specific
objects or situations. Even a color name, for example, may be
used, not for many things of the same color, but only for certain
objects. Thus, green may be thought of only as the color of grass
or of a certain hat or of a book. Words become names for individual things, instead of for groups of similar things. Asked for definitions of words, and given the word "book," the response was, "It
depends what book you are referring to." For "table," a patient
answered: "What kind of table? A wooden table, a porcelain
table, a surgical table, or a table you want to have a meal on?"
The larger meanings of things have vanished, it appears; the
world has become filled with "this alone" and "that in itself."

It looks here as though disorder has gone beyond anything
that can be linked with anxiety or guilt or personal problems, and
that it has begun to involve processes which have nothing to do
with emotional conflicts. The complexion of the mystery may
change a bit, however, if we return again to the idea that this
form of the illness represents not so much a *loss* of the usual meanings of things, as a *tendency to withdraw* from these meanings.
This phase of the schizophrenic flight from reality may be an attempt to get and to keep as close as possible to the most elementary way of viewing the world. In some respects it might be regarded as child-like. The schizophrenic seems to be seeking the

single, simple experience; he seems to be trying to see the world in a concrete unorganized way, and to leave behind all the more complex, more abstract, more adult meanings of things. His thinking is closer to sensation, closer to that characteristic of primitive peoples. It is a shallower way of perceiving; it is "of and for the moment."

The following account of one person's observations on the effects of alcohol may give a glimpse of this quality of schizophrenic thought: "I think that what led to my drinking was that without it I was never able to enter into anything fully—that is, anything but my work and my worries. I could never give myself up to the moment. Always there was a tension in the background. There was the feeling: I haven't got time for this; there are too many things waiting for me, too many things threatening. Personal problems still nagging at me. All the things I hadn't done, and things I felt guilty about. All the old pains and frustrations.

"Well, a few drinks would lift all that away from me. All the old thoughts were gone, about how mixed up I was and how dissatisfied I was with myself. I wouldn't think much. I guess I was what you call 'detached.' It was like being a child, just looking at colors, hearing sounds, and watching people. All this was because *the load was off. The load of the past and the load of the future. It was living just for the moment, and for the sensation, and not thinking.* I guess you could say that while the drinks lasted *everything was simplified.* I guess you could call it kind of brainless too. Sometimes I'd feel a bit foolish, enjoying things this way."

It is plain that this observer managed to shut out, for a while, the pressure of conflict and painful emotion by what amounted to a *reduction* of experience to the concrete present. He escaped from the larger meanings of things, and especially from the personalized meanings. A reduction of experience in the schizophrenic, of a perhaps comparable kind, may serve a similar purpose. To live only in the surface impressions of each moment is to exclude a very large part of life and of one's self, but if this part contains somewhere a nucleus of anxiety, of frustration or of guilt, the sacrifice becomes to some degree understandable.

Possibly the nearest that mentally well people ever get to such a state of mind would be in seeking diversion from worrisome problems, anxious thoughts, grief or remorse by becoming absorbed in some tangible activity (for example, painting, woodworking, ceramics), by directing attention *toward* objects and *away from* people, into the inanimate, and away from all personalized meanings.

language may be private

The occasional resemblance of schizophrenic language to a personal idiom has been mentioned. It has been described as a tendency to use words less as a public tool of communication and more as a private code-speech, addressed as much or more to the self as to others. It is often suggested that what we have here is not a breakdown of the language function, but a marked exaggeration of an occasional feature of normal speech, namely, the development of individualized, or eccentric, habits of expression. This particular facet of the "language symptom" deserves further discussion, since it is importantly related to a fundamental feature of schizophrenic behavior touched upon earlier.

One of the commonest markings of the personality which may later become schizophrenic is an inclination to *withdraw from contacts with others,* to become a social isolationist, a non-mixer, an outsider. The psychological meaning of this movement of behavior will be treated in the chapter to follow. At this point it is enough to stress the consequences of such behavior in developing the ability to communicate effectively with others through spoken language.

An extremely vital part of the process of growing up, for all of us, is learning to convey our thoughts and feelings to others. The shut-in, going his solitary way, does not get adequate practice in expressing himself to others, in expressing himself, that is, in a way that enables others to understand him. His withdrawal confirms him, instead, in a tendency that has been observed in the language development of the normal child.

There is evidence that the effort to express thoughts in such a way as to make them understood by others is often absent in young children of five or six years. The reason for this is that the child has as yet no real wish to communicate with others; ". . . each child, whether he is trying to explain his own thoughts or to understand those of others, is shut up in his own point of view."

The child first talks largely for himself. He is wrapped up in his own interests. He is not really trying to converse. When he begins to do so he is very careless of logic. People will find him difficult to understand. He does not take the other person's point of view. He simply takes it for granted that he will be understood, and this is because children "are perpetually surrounded by adults who not only know much more than they do, but who also do everything in their power to understand them and who even anticipate their thoughts and their desires." The child is therefore under little necessity to adjust his language to the needs of his listener until the time comes when he must make himself clear to other children.*

The child's habit of assuming that his listener understands him regardless of the inadequacy of his speech is obviously not favorable to good communication. As the child grows up he discovers that he *must*, if he is to be understood, put his thoughts into the form that we call a logical order. This logic that is normally present in our speech and thinking and that is often so

---

* It may be mentioned that this kind of experience with adults may suggest to the child that others can read his thoughts, and it seems possible that this may be related to a symptom frequently found in schizophrenics, the conviction that people know what is present in their minds. Thus, a very immature schizophrenic girl was often impatient under question by the writer because she believed that he must already know the answers to his questions; she thought he must be "putting on an act" of ignorance, and she found this quite irritating.

lacking in the language of the schizophrenic is something we achieve through years of attempting to express our thoughts in such a way that others will grasp them. The way we finally learn to think, and therefore to talk, is largely a product of social experience that forces us to use the words others use *with the same meanings and in the same way that others use them.*

It is apparent, then, what may happen when a child develops, for whatever reason (for example, timidity, or unpleasant experiences with other children) a tendency to withdraw. His speech habits will tend to retain their childish, egocentric character. He will communicate poorly. While all of us, doubtless, understand our own thoughts better than we convey them to others, this will be true to a much greater degree of such a child. If he becomes a daydreamer as well as a solitary, as is probable, he will be likely, moreover, to have little impulse to express himself effectively to others. As he builds a private world of imaginary gratifications he will come to lack the desire as well as the ability to make himself understood.

Illustrations of some of the peculiarities of schizophrenic thought and speech have been seen as defenses against painful emotions, as trends of preoccupation, as a kind of emotionalized (or "primitive") logic, as a narrowing of thought and perception to immediate and concrete levels, and as the formation of highly individualized speech habits.

While our emphasis has been on the defensive character of these phenomena, it is clear that this is not the entire story. There is a positive side of the matter, too, when, by means of nonrational "logic," a need is satisfied, or some desire is indulged. In other ways as well such behavior has its *gratifications,* and one observer has remarked that the schizophrenic "seems to enjoy the fact that you do not understand him." [8]

It is now time to attempt an answer to a basic question that has been hovering in the background of all our discussion of defensive delusions, of defensive language peculiarities and of defensive withdrawal behavior. While in some of the cases at least, a partial answer has been given, a more comprehensive and fundamental understanding is needed of *what it is* the schizophrenic is defending, and *why* defense has come to loom so large in his approach to life.

10. what is

schizophrenia?

A sampling of schizophrenic behavior has been presented in the foregoing chapters. These cases have been offered as illustrations rather than as a complete survey, since this book is not a treatise on the subject. Certain types of the disorder have not yet, in fact, been mentioned at all. For illustration it seemed best to offer, in some instances, only a few features of a case.

Can we find, in this variety of behavior pictures, an inner core of meaning that will make them understandable? Is there, despite the differences, an inner likeness that will help us to tell what this illness really is?

Little can be said about it that will apply to *all* schizophrenics, but important things can be said that apply to a great many. The tendency to withdraw was mentioned earlier. While not always present, it is very common. The schizophrenic shows, with great frequency, clear signs of discomfort in social contacts and a marked tendency to avoid them. He may complain of loneliness, yet he prefers to be alone. He feels tense in the presence of others, and sometimes even with those familiar to him. Such avoidance is especially marked in competitive situations. Relationships already established may show diminishing warmth; withdrawal is, of course, basically *emotional*.

Along with the withdrawal there is often a tendency toward limitation of activities. There is a narrowing down of living. Desire for novelty and for diversity of experience weakens. There is growing apathy and lack of zest. As if by a kind of spiritual parsimony the victim cuts down on his contacts. An intelligent schizophrenic girl asked for some routine hospital work. She was advised that it might seem monotonous to a person of her capacities. She replied: "I like monotony. I can relax better." She might have added, "I feel safer that way."

Withdrawal may be gradual, or more or less sudden. It often begins during adolescence, sometimes earlier. It is to be seen, in any event, as no more than the outward sign of an inner change.

Where it is possible to find a stressful event that looks like the cause of the emotional change, the event is very often not an uncommon one. Usually it may safely be supposed that a great many people have met and survived such stresses without any marked disturbance. What makes the difference in response between those who survive and those who break?

What makes this difference is sensitivity to a certain *kind* of stress. This sensitivity is finally traceable to experiences in very early life which have given rise to intense *anxiety*. These experiences may be few or many; they may be remembered or forgotten. The special sensitiveness to the original anxiety-arousing situation may, in some individuals, be overlaid by other experiences and lie dormant for many years, then come explosively into the open under exceptional pressures. When, in later life, they react to stress with panic, or with anxiety that may fairly be judged as too great for the danger, their behavior may be seen as a revival of this "hibernating" emotional condition. In other persons, however, the anxiety may apparently be more or less conscious from the beginning, and even lead to the development of a distinctive kind of personality.

How do our cases support the idea that anxiety is the central and deep-lying source of schizophrenic illness? Sometimes the evidence is clear and direct. In Martha, for example, anxiety was often close to the surface. She was a dependent person who needed a guide and helper. The daily evidence she was able to find that her life was being planned for her was a shield from the fear of feeling utterly alone. Anxiety played a similar role in the case of the dependent boy, Max, who sought comfort in the belief that "helpers" were about, that he was among friends.

It is a far cry, it would seem, from the case of Florrie, or the "Old Maid," or Florence (with her notions of enforced prostitution), to that of Daniel Schreber. Yet the acute conflicts that led to "voices" and to delusions were all linked with anxiety concerning sex. The symptom spared each one from the direct owning of unacceptable impulses or conduct. Florrie repressed her guilt. Ada and Florence dodged it by pointing the accusing finger elsewhere. Schreber avoided it by glorifying his sensuality as an act of God.

In each of these people the build of character was such that forbidden impulses or behavior would have called forth, but for the symptom, an acutely anxious shame. The relation between guilt and anxiety appears to be well established. The basic setting in which all of us learn the meaning of guilt is that of punishment, disapproval or rejection.

There are several ways in which anxiety is aroused by guilt. There is, of course, the fear of physical punishment. More important is the fear of social punishment—that is, of censure, of loss of acceptance or respect. There is also the fear of the catastrophic damage to morale, to pride, the spiritual collapse that may come when one is confronted with unmistakable evidence of a deeply humiliating part of one's self. Again, the anxiety connected with guilt may have a religious basis. It may be the fear of divine retribution. Thus, a patient confessed that her anxiety to avoid any injury to others was entirely a concern about her own spiritual status: "It was completely selfish . . . it was my own soul's purity I was worried about."

A prominent feature of some of our cases is *hostility*. This was best seen in Willie, whose personality was charged with it, and again in Ada and in Marcella, who managed to believe they were persecuted in order to have an excuse for vengeful feelings. In the latter two, it was especially clear that the hostility was a reaction to rejection, and that rejection was linked with anxiety. The close relationship between hostility and anxiety has been well stated by May: anxiety is an extremely painful experience, and therefore arouses strong resentment toward those responsible for arousing it in us. To be dependent upon someone and helpless without him, for example, will cause us to feel angry toward him when we are frustrated in our needs. Thus, even the loved parent may become the object of the child's rage when its desires are blocked.

It has often been pointed out, moreover, that such hostility breeds further anxiety in that we risk losing the one we need when we vent such feeling upon him. As one writer put it: "When you want people to like you and when at the same time you are angry with them, the situation is peculiarly frustrating." [1] Marcella, for example, was anxious about people liking her when she moved into a new neighborhood. Because of her sensitivity and her habit of reading signs of dislike in others, she soon perceived slights and offenses. To these she reacted with angry outbursts. This increased her anxiety, since she knew these outbursts would strengthen the feeling against her.

The cases reviewed all point, therefore, in the same direction; namely, toward anxiety as their central core and source. The behavior of our schizophrenics is to be seen, in other words, either as anxiety nakedly revealed, or as a means of avoiding anxiety, or as anger aroused by a cause of anxiety. It remains, now, to tell more exactly *what kind of anxiety* this is; to tell where it comes from, and why certain people appear to have much more of it than others.

a certain kind of anxiety

Each of us has his own way or style of responding or relating to others. We may be typically open and receptive, or aloof and wary. We may be relaxed and comfortable, or stiff and tense. We also have our own way of regarding ourselves in relation to others. We may feel confident of acceptance wherever we go or we may feel habitually doubtful or guarded or cautious, or we may habitually get set for what we feel will be possible or probable rejection.

How does each person come to have his own particular way of feeling toward people, and toward himself? We would expect, certainly, that the kind of experience he has previously had *with* people would be of first importance. It is a familiar fact, moreover, that certain experiences leave deeper and more lasting effects than others. For example, a girl may find that her first love affair has made so sharp and profound an impression as to color, for many years, all of her reactions to men. She may find that its effect upon her confidence or upon her standards of what is desirable in a mate is a long-lasting or even a permanent one. Or, again, a man who is victimized in an important business dealing with a particular person may become suspicious, bitter and cynical of *every* new acquaintance for a long while. Certain experiences with certain people may be tremendously vital in molding the quality of our social feelings in general.

There are, of course, a great many possibilities as to which people may be influential, and why, and what kinds of imprints they may leave behind them. It appears to be fairly well agreed by present-day psychologists and psychiatrists, however, that with regard to the all-important feelings which relate to acceptance of and respect for others, and to acceptance of and respect for one's self, the equally all-important persons are most likely to be one's parents.

For this great importance it is obvious that there are several reasons. Parents are the *first* persons with whom we have continuous close contact. They are, for a long while, almost the *sole* representatives of the race to which we belong, therefore our one and only "sample" of humankind. They make our first social world for us, and the kind of people they are make the kind of world it must be. There will be a tendency, moreover, to feel toward others as we feel toward them. They are the criterion.

For the growth of the fundamental traits of self-liking and self-respect, the most vital experience for the child is the way his parents affect his feeling about his own worth. Treatment that assures him that he is loved by them and is precious to them lays the foundation for what will later be called his self-esteem. If they approve of him, he will approve of himself. In learning from them how they value him, he learns how to value himself. His parents, doubtless usually without awareness of what they are doing, are teaching him how to appraise himself. The habitual feelings that arise from the most favorable parental treatment are the basis of what is often termed "emotional security."

From this it is easy to surmise the effects of treatment in which these qualities are lacking. Periodic disapproval is, of course, necessary to training, but if disapproval is rarely or never offset by praise, and if it tends to be applied to the child's entire self, rather than to his behavior, the formation of a subnormal level of confidence begins. Repeated disparagement, belittlement and rejection lay the foundation for a chronically lowered esteem of the self. The child is learning what he is worth. The image he forms of himself is a direct reflection of what he reads in the eyes of his parents.

Most important of all is the emotional effect of this experience of repeated disapproval. To be rejected by a person who is almost the whole of one's world, the sole provider not only of all physical comfort and satisfactions but of all wellbeing and security, can be nothing less than catastrophic. The result is a certain kind of anxiety. This *kind* of anxiety is of exceedingly great importance in relation to later mental illness. It is not to be compared with the fear of threatening situations or of specific dangers. It engulfs the entire self. Patients who can recall it have described it in terms of overwhelming panic. They may say: "I just felt completely and utterly *lost*."

From the intensity of such anxiety the strength of the child's dependent need of his parents may be surmised. So great is this need that he *must* believe in their goodness. Sometimes, in fact, a child who has been harshly treated will insist upon his own badness in order to retain his belief that his parents are good, that they are really kind.

Many students of the background of mental illness agree that the most important of the child's reactions to parental rejection is this catastrophic and overwhelming anxiety. There is, however, a further possibility: the child may react to rejection with some degree of resentment or hostility. Anxiety may dominate, with hostility only occasional, but sometimes it becomes a prominent feature of the emotional effects of parental treatment. One of the commonest conflicts found deep in the personality of the schizophrenic is that between anxiety and hostility. Hostility may emerge, in some instances, as the most conspicuous feature of the reaction to the parents, even though anxiety may be detectable close beneath the surface.

What makes this difference in the effect of parental disapproval? There are those who believe that the particular *way* the child reacts will depend on the particular *kind* of treatment adopted by the parents. Granted the undoubted truth of this, allowance must also be made for deep-lying differences in emotional temperament. There may be inherited factors that have some part in what makes the difference between the child who reacts to harsh treatment mainly with anxiety and submissiveness (like Gus), and the child who responds mainly with hostility (like Willie).

Given the basic fact of childhood anxiety, the question then becomes: how does this kind of anxiety affect development? What kind of personality results when sensitivity about social acceptance is intense enough and painful enough to become a major influence upon the growth process?

the schizoid personality

In this section a certain kind of personality is to be described. It is important to stress at the outset that this personality is not doomed to schizophrenia. Nor is possession of any of the traits to be noted a symptom of the beginnings of the illness. A person may be schizoid much of his life without becoming schizophrenic, (and some schizophrenics have *not* been schizoid). People who develop the illness have, nevertheless, so often been previously schizoid to some degree that an important key to its meaning may be found here.

A person with a physical wound soon learns to guard himself in such a way as to protect the painful part of his body. He "favors" the wounded member, and he avoids situations or movements that are likely to jar or bruise it.

The anxiety that comes from rejection by the person who is, for a while, the entire world, and who embodies all safety, comfort and security, may be one of the most agonizing experiences a child can have. Its repetition must result in a high degree of sensitivity. The child becomes *set* to perceive the signs and markings of disapproval in others as well as in his parents. He becomes highly attentive to those features of social situations—to fleeting facial expressions, to inflections and tones of voice—which convey, even in the slightest degree, the threat of non-acceptance, of slights and disparagement.

In ordinary conversations we commonly do not think to any great extent about ourselves. We certainly do not think continually, as we talk, of how the other is reacting to our various qualities, or how we are affecting him with regard to his approval or disapproval. We are thinking, mainly, of a topic of mutual interest. But for an *insecure* person such a relationship may be strongly charged with a *personalized* quality. Anyone who confronts him will be closely observed for every slightest sign that may give a clue to how far they accept him, respect him, like or dislike him. Every social situation becomes a test and a challenge. In every contact the question foremost is: How much or how little does this person think of me? How does he appraise my value as a human being? Is he attracted or repelled?

Such a frame of mind will be linked with anxiety for a person who has repeatedly experienced the hurts of injury to the self. The logical outcome of this state of mind is to seek protective avoidance of social contacts. But the high priority need to protect the self from injury may go much beyond this. It may determine the build of the entire personality. This is as natural an effect of the anxiety as the burnt child's reaction to the candle flame. In the literature of schizophrenia this generalized response to painful social experience is summed up in the term "withdrawal." Again and again in the case histories we come upon references to increasing avoidance behavior during the early period of illness. For example: "After dinner she usually went up to her room and stayed there all evening, staring out the window." Again: "When visitors called, he usually went to his room and stayed until they were gone." In another case: "Rather than pass people on a sidewalk he would cross the street and walk on the other side. This was true even of people he seemed to like. . . . On summer evenings, when he came home from work and people would be on the porches, he'd take a path through the backyards to avoid having to say 'hello' so many times. When he had to do this he'd call it 'running the gauntlet.'"

Such avoidance behavior means loneliness, and loneliness often breeds depression, but it also means the kind of *safety* that is needed, and for this the price is not too great. A young patient once told me his dream was to live alone some day in a one-room cabin, far in the suburbs, with perhaps a half-acre for some gardening. He emphasized how few and simple his needs were. Every few months he might work "a week or two" in a factory for funds he might need. It would be, he thought, a "cosy little life."

These are the people who become adept at avoiding emotional entanglements. They tend to be aloof in their feelings as well as in physical distance from others. Familiar to all those who have worked with the schizoid individual is the difficulty of "getting close" to him in therapy interview. He is guarded and wary, and often so repressed as to seem entirely without feelings. This is "that loss of personal *rapport*, that loss of sympathetic contact . . . that appearance of complete indifference to persons, which is the most characteristic symptom of the disorder."

Yet this indifference is but a protective shield, and beneath the surface coldness there lies, as many observers assure us, no vacuum, but a sensitivity so great that only by such armoring can even the minimum of social intercourse be tolerated. Thus, "in the schizoid there is no lack or weakness of the self-affects, the emotions and impulses of the sentiment of self-regard . . . rather, the self-affects are strong and . . . even in the early but well-marked stages of schizophrenia, they are unduly active . . ."

A recent writer has well described the defenses erected by the schizoid personality against the anxieties he risks in face-to-face relationships. He is the sort of person who prefers to write a letter rather than to telephone or make a personal call. As a student he is more comfortable with books than with a teacher, and so learns more from solitary reading than in the classroom. He tends to be a poor loser at games, for a loss touches his over-sensitized complex of inadequacy feeling; he has, in one sense or another, "lost" too many times already, and cannot afford more losses.

Another expression of the defensive tendency may be a preference for ideas as against action, seen in prolonged preoccupation with *making plans* as against taking concrete steps toward a goal. Here we find also, occasionally, what amounts to a "search for safety" in religion. A schizoid boy of 22, with little previous interest in religion, began to talk of entering a monastery following an experience of acute anxiety. A girl of very insecure family background, and low in confidence, gained great assurance and purpose in adopting one of the dogmatic evangelical religions in which she was enabled to feel that she was one of the "select," and to talk glibly in prescribed formulas.

It has been remarked that the schizoid tends to be lacking in humor, for he takes himself too seriously to be able to view himself in the way that permits laughter. "In order to be humorous, a man must stand a little apart from himself, must view himself objectively as a specimen of humanity that shares its weaknesses and is liable to its common failures and shortcomings." The schizoid is too close, habitually, to his own failures and shortcomings, and feels them too sharply. The relaxation that humor requires is difficult for him.

Being self-conscious, unsure of himself and uncomfortable with others, the schizoid finds reality too often painful and frustrating. He therefore tends to gratify himself with fantasies. He is inclined to spend much time in imaginary experiences in which he obtains partial satisfaction of his longings. Though such fantasies are thin, milk and water substitutes for the real thing, they offer easy enjoyments. With such resources at hand, he tends to become apathetic about action. One result of this is a narrowing of external interests and of socializing activities. Repeatedly, in the case histories of the schizoid child, there are references to poor relationships with other children, a rarity of close friendships. Recreation tends to be solitary. Communications are poor with family members; the child is inclined to be close-mouthed, to keep his troubles to himself.

A consequence of withdrawal is a failure to develop normal *social skills*, that is, effortless and enjoyable ways of getting along with others, of understanding them, and of dealing with them. The schizoid's lack of confidence in the various ways of social living is really quite logical, for he has not learned, does not "know the ropes" in these matters. He fears blunders and awkwardness, and for good reason. So the original crippling of his confidence in the basic family setting leads to avoidances. The avoidances perpetuate the condition, and so the circle is complete.

Another effect of withdrawal is related to the earlier discussion of the way in which delusions come about. A central question was: Granted that a delusion may be a means of satisfying some strong need, how is it possible to retain a false belief in the face of contradictory facts? Delusions which involve false ideas about the physical world may be explained in part by ignorance of the facts and laws of natural phenomena. Delusions about people and about one's self in relation to people, are similarly related to the amount and kinds of knowledge acquired about behavior.

An extremely important use of such knowledge is to serve as a *corrective* for certain kinds of thoughts about the self, and about people. Such thoughts represent the individual's naive, "inexperienced" image of the sort of person he is. At times they may border on fantasy. We have all, of course, indulged in such enjoyable flights. In them we envision roles we would like to play, the way we would have others regard us, and the kind of people others would have to be in order to behave as we wish.

In fantasy such ideas are shaped mainly by what we want. A normal part of growing up lies in the progressive *revision* of these ideas toward more realistic ways of thinking. The "facts of life" must be learned with regard to various personal ambitions, with respect to how attractive one's personality is to men and women, and for what traits one is most respected, and whether one is to be a leader or a follower, etc. For this kind of learning a certain minimum amount of experience with people is imperative. Without it there can be no check upon goals, no standard by which to rate one's ambitions, or to measure one's assets. Without this minimum of experience a person does not discover his limits. He does not learn what he looks like in the eyes of others, or what he can expect of others in their responses to him. He cannot, without it, value himself properly because he knows too little of others to have a criterion.

By thus avoiding, through withdrawal, opportunities for this kind of social correction, the schizoid remains free to make a self-picture colored by his fantasies. Add to this that his skill in perceiving the attitudes of others must remain poor, and the way is clear for a variety of *mis-readings* of their responses toward him. If feelings of guilt and inadequacy are prominent, he may be inclined to find derogatory meanings, accusations, etc., in what he hears. Or, if he has developed an exaggerated notion of his abilities, he may mistake a helpful criticism for jealousy.

An effort to offer correctives may, in fact, be rather thankless. A schizoid boy once revealed to me some observations he had made on word similarities and meanings, in which he believed he saw a possible theory of the origin of language. While the observations were very superficial and elementary, he was greatly impressed by what he felt was a rather profound insight.

He became hotly resentful when obvious weaknesses in his "important discovery" were pointed out to him.

Again, a maladjusted and rather seclusive college freshman had developed an unrealistic and impractical plan for a career which appeared to him as a relatively easy way to considerable prestige. His father arranged an appointment for him with a vocational counselor to help convince his son of the defect in his plan. The student did not keep the appointment, and became quite irritable when pressed to do so. It was clear that he did not want to risk possible damage to his enjoyable semi-fantasy.

In summary, what has so far been described is a certain kind of *personality* rather than a mental illness. It is a personality distinguished by defenses. Some of these are easy to recognize; some are not at all apparent. Their purpose is to protect a deep central core of sensitivity to anxiety, implanted in early life by experiences with parents, or with parent-figures. These experiences have left the child unsure of his worth and his acceptance. He continues, in other words, to respond to *all* people, to some degree, as he learned to respond to his parents. In his social relations he might be said to be *arrested* at the "parental level" of development.

It should be said again that such a personality need not become schizophrenic. Many such people continue to show the traits described without progressing any further toward disorder. They may lead limited, and perhaps not very happy lives, but not abnormal ones as this term is commonly understood. They will be regarded as reserved and aloof, and they may even occasionally impress some as feeling "superior" because of their tendency to keep others at a distance.

If a closer acquaintance can be managed, it will be discovered that the aloofness is a cover for timidity, that beneath the apparent self-sufficiency is a need and a loneliness which makes an ironic contrast with the mask they wear. Strong as the impulse to open up to others may be, the fear of rebuff is stronger. If a chance encounter under favorable circumstances should penetrate the defenses and they feel the beginnings of an invasion of their emotional life by another, it is likely that the unaccustomed experience will carry too great a threat; anxiety will rise to a pitch that compels a flight to social safety. They return to their spiritual cloister like the captive circus animal whose cage door was sprung open in a wreck, and who turned back after a few diffident steps toward freedom.

from schizoid to schizophrenic

Beginning with this withdrawn, shut-in kind of personality, the journey into schizophrenia is usually described as hinging upon a crisis of some sort. This may be one of the major turning-point events or phases of normal living, such as the advent of adolescence, prospective marriage, the birth of a child. A vocational challenge, or a crucial failure in occupation may be central, or the death of someone close, a broken engagement, a humiliating blunder, or a severe conflict with a parent. The critical event may represent a step forward toward independence, or into an unknown region of experience. For the self-doubting, apprehensive and insecure person it is seen as a *test* situation. In some way he is "on the spot." His resources, competence, his *value*, are to be appraised. He faces what is, in effect, a time of judgment. The essence of the crisis is the arousal of intense anxiety by what affects him as a severe threat to, or damage of, whatever sense of personal adequacy he has managed to achieve.

The situations that lead to this illness are, as several writers have stressed, those that suddenly cause violent injury to the self-esteem. As the usual defenses, or "ways out," fail, one after another, the anxiety finally approaches panic intensity. This ultimate anxiety then evokes the ultimate defense—that of mental disorder.

It is important to make strongly the point that to induce the illness, a stress must be something that affects a person in *a particular way*. It must shake him at the heart and center of his personality. Neither the kind nor the intensity of whatever happens in the emotional life is as important as whether it strikes at the backbone of morale and the feelings of personal worth. The schizoid is sensitized to certain kinds of situations and experiences, but not to all.

The point may be illustrated with an experience reported by a student. Desire to become successful in literature was his greatest personal ambition. All else was secondary. He had submitted a short story to a magazine and received a favorable preliminary report on it. During a period of several weeks following this, a number of events occurred that would ordinarily be considered as shocks. He was involved in a rather bad automobile accident. He failed to be invited to join a fraternity he was interested in. Finally, his father became seriously ill. The student was able to take these blows in stride. He was himself somewhat surprised, in fact, at his quick recoveries from each of them. He realized that the vital lift to his literary hopes was largely responsible. Regarding his rejection by the fraternity he said: "That one letter from the editor meant more to me than what all those fellows in the 'frat' thought of me."

When, however, he was notified that after reconsideration his story was not to be published, he became profoundly depressed; his "spirit broke"; his school grades, which had been steady, now suffered badly. The main support on which depended his deepest feeling of personal worth had now given way. It was here that his greatest vulnerability lay.

The personality of the schizoid may similarly be shaken much more by some situations than by others. His special vulnerability is affected by any situation which touches his *basic confidence.* In general it can be said that sharp downward steps on the path to schizophrenia occur in connection with events that lower the patient's already feeble self-esteem or challenge in some way his adequacy. Anything that makes him feel . . . less competent than he already thinks himself to be, has a devastating effect ." [2]

There will be stresses, then, that the schizoid person may be

expected to survive as well as anyone else. Misfortunes affecting his professional and economic well-being, or his health and
family affairs, may not upset him beyond the normal if they involve no issues connected with the major supports of his morale.
It has often been pointed out that, at times of nationwide ordeal
and calamity (for example, business depressions, war-time,
etc.), there is no increase in the amount of schizophrenic illness.
While these shocks may bring great distress, they are impersonal.
They do not touch feelings of adequacy in any way. They are
the kind of thing that "can happen to anybody." In considering
an experience as a factor in this mental disorder, therefore, the
important thing is not so much the event itself as its personal
meaning to the individual.

The break into illness may come at some one of the
challenge-points mentioned. Or it may come later, at a time when
the individual is already beginning to falter under the stress. Or
still later, when he has, with a fair degree of conclusiveness, failed
to "pass his test," that is, when he has failed to get his promotion,
or to make the grade in school, or when he has lost his job, or his
sweetheart, or when his marriage has foundered.

During the period of peak stress he does his best to master
his mounting anxiety. He is trying to hang on. The strain may
show in irritability, or inability to concentrate. He may become
preoccupied, complain of fatigue, loss of appetite, sleeplessness.

The culminating experience of acute anxiety may be to some
degree intelligible to anyone who has known a moment of
panic, and who can recall, perhaps, that he became confused,
that his thinking was disorganized, his speech incoherent. He
may even recall that he felt lost, that the world became threatening, even a bit unreal.

Out of this experience may develop the beginnings of
delusion-formation when the patient perceives a way of thinking
that offers an escape—a solution for his problem. (A familiar
example of this is the case in which, confronted by a major professional setback in achievement, he manages to find grounds for
tracing it to the resentful maneuvers of rivals rather than to per-

sonal failure.) Or the anxiety may culminate in a paralysis of behavior in which the patient becomes immobile. He may become
apathetic, stuporous or mute.

Again, the beginnings of disorder may be characterized by a
variety of misinterpretations of external events, by grandiose
ideas, by the kind of illogical thinking described in Chapter 8,
and sometimes by a flooding of the mind with vivid memory images out of long-past periods of life.

On the other hand, as will later be seen, the beginning may
be much more gradual; the illness may develop over a period of
years, and in the absence of any discoverable emotional crisis, or
any unusual stress of circumstances.

the symptom as a defense

Now that a fairly definite view as to the emotional basis of
this commonest of all mental illnesses has been outlined, it may
be well to survey its applications, that is, to see how much it
helps in understanding the behavior so far described.

It is clear that anxiety concerning acceptance by others and
by one's self is closely related to the kind of personal crises, culminating in a state of panic, which was described in Chapter 8
and emphasized in Boisen's account of the inner experiences in
schizophrenia. It is obvious too that anxiety so essentially bound
up with social contacts should lead to the fundamental symptom
of withdrawal.

Above all, anxiety seeks defense. For an understanding of
the behavior of the schizophrenic the concept of defense is central. As in the schizoid the distinctive *traits of personality* may
be seen as protective in function, so in the schizophrenic a great
many of the *symptoms of illness* represent shields against anxiety.
These range from small things, like the wordy evasive maneuvers
that parry a question, to big things, like an elaborate and well-
constructed delusional system. Among our cases the protective

function of the symptom was most clearly seen, perhaps, in Florrie, in Marilyn, in Schreber, in Ada, and in Harold, with his "poisoned heart."

Several ways in which the peculiarities of schizophrenic language may be seen as defensive were suggested in Chapter 9. The patient moves away, verbally, from painful topics. He uses speech "for counteracting his feelings of insecurity among other people." He uses it, again, "to bolster his own feeble sense of security like the man who talks loudly in the dark, trying to drown out his anxiety by the sound of his own voice." The tendency toward concreteness, as earlier illustrated, has also been considered as a fundamental protective alteration of the thought processes.

It has long been recognized that the schizophrenic personality is often conspicuously immature. The dependencies founded in childhood are especially prominent. A striking fact is the persistence, from early life far into adulthood, of the effects of certain kinds of experience.

The insecure person, low in confidence, is likely to be handicapped severely in becoming self-reliant. If one of the meanings of "growing up" is the development of independent resourcefulness, we will expect that a person chronically anxious about his adequacy will be slowed up in his progress toward maturity. Anxiety, in inhibiting initiative, will retard this phase of mental growth.

All of us are, of course, the products of all that has happened to us, but we *continue* to change. Today's new challenges may cause us to discard or alter much of what was learned yesterday. The schizophrenic seems to be, to an unusual degree, a creature of his own past. He is less able to outgrow the emotions of childhood and of youth. "Some people," said a highly intelligent schizophrenic woman, "just can't live beyond what has happened to them." Another patient talked, again and again, of ". . . this enormous past weighing me down." Another said: "I think I could forget some of the things my father did . . . if my *feelings* would let me. It's my feelings that can't seem to forget."

A recent writer refers to "the almost irresistible impulse of the schizophrenic patient to return again and again to his mother . . ." [3]

A schizoid "boy" of twenty-eight upset his family considerably by pleading with his father for what amounted to permission to have extramarital sex relations with a girl. Without permission of his parents he would feel too guilty, he said, to indulge himself. His arguments were of the kind that might fairly normally have been used, by many youths, in an attempt to justify such sexual freedom (though hardly to his parents!). Instead of acting upon these arguments independently, however, he felt that he must have a parental "release." Rather than attempt to break the bonds of dependency he felt forced to try—very unrealistically, in view of the strictness of his parents—to convert them to permissiveness.

An unusually clear example is that of Kafka, who struggled throughout life to overcome the powerful feelings of self-rejection and unworthiness traceable to childhood treatment by his father. Despite high intelligence and insight capacity and the many testimonials he received as an adult to his extraordinary individual worth, he seems to have remained, in this region of his emotional life, a child.

In discussions of mental illness there is often a reference to the possibility that certain people are more susceptible to disorder than others. Such a tendency is perhaps most commonly called a "predisposition." It suggests that certain individuals have, somehow, what amounts to a headstart toward mental disturbance, even before anything actually happens to them.

In none of our schizophrenics can we say that any single incident or stress has *alone* been responsible for the onset of illness. What we find, instead, is that a certain kind of personality, molded by certain kinds of experiences and upbringing, has been affected in an extraordinary way by fairly ordinary stresses.

In our account of the persecution complex, the effect of acute anxiety in distorting perception was illustrated in the case of the man who believed himself pursued by gangsters he had offended while intoxicated. Here a delusion became established by progressive mis-readings of people's behavior. While the early errors might be understood by way of normal anxiety, the exaggerated behavior that finally developed suggests that anxiety from a deeper source must have been aroused.

In the case of Florrie, and of several others included in our survey, a similar question may be raised. Why was guilt so distressing an experience? That Florrie's anxiety centered upon social disapproval of her sex behavior was evident. A person with an anxiety complex of the kind we are here concerned with may certainly be over-sensitized to guilt reactions. If fear of rejection was at times acute in Florrie's girlhood, the excessive anxiety occasioned by her later guilt becomes easily intelligible.*

In these cases, it may be, the true predisposing factor is parental rejection, which, by way of anxiety, prepares an over-reaction to guilt. In such instances the idea of the schizophrenic reaction as a disturbance traceable to early life, and re-aroused by later experiences, helps to enlighten the "panic" phenomenon earlier discussed. The view gains support from cases in which the reaction to an adult experience appears as excessive and irrational, in which the history reveals general factors, such as the personality of a parent, which may be related to this excessive reaction, and finally in which specific incidents are recoverable which demonstrate the connection between the experience and the emotion.

On the whole, and looking backward over our survey, it appears that the anxiety principle (that is, the anxiety related to acceptance by the self and by others) is quite versatile in its

---

* Florrie reacted to her guilty behavior as a "good" girl should, which may be related to the occasional reports of the notable docility and obedience of children who become schizophrenic. Repeatedly, evidence appears that rejection-anxiety explains the overly submissive child (e.g., "I never had to spank her. Just one word, and the tears would come."). That the very "good" child may also have nervous habits, night terrors and other indications that all is not well, has been noted by Hill.[4] May points out that it is rejection, not in itself, but when "covered over with pretense of love and concern" that breeds anxiety.[5] To this may be added that the dependency-bond may be deeper in some children than others.

applications. This is in part because so many different things are tied up with the self-appraisal. Successes and failures of many kinds affect it. The jolt to morale may come, as we have seen, by way of a professional failure, or a failure in social relationships, a failure in sexual adequacy or a failure in masculinity. A frustration or defeat of the drive toward independence may be central. Seemingly small things may be large in effect; it is the personal meaning rather than the absolute size of an incident that counts. Morale at its lowest ebb, or when extremely unstable, may easily collapse at a prick. A patient who burst into tears when a mop, which he had been handling clumsily, was taken from him, sobbed: "I can't even do *that* right."

the symptom as fulfillment

A second meaning of the schizophrenic disorder was earlier touched upon. The symptom may be a *direct* expression of an emotional state, as when anxiety, or guilt or hostility leads to delusional interpretations or to chronic personality tendencies. Here the individual is at the mercy of the dominant emotion, overwhelmed by it, his perceptions colored and distorted. In these cases we cannot say that the symptom is purposive, that in some way it meets a need. It represents simply the "organism in pain" from the misfortunes of development and of experience.

Little has been said of a third class of symptoms. In none of our case illustrations has it been prominent, although lightly touched upon. Schreber's exaggerated idea of his own importance was mentioned, a notion which must surely have been gratifying to him. The patient who believed herself the Virgin Mary needed an escape from her feeling of sinfulness, but she must likewise have experienced gratification in the fulfillment of her idealized dream of sainthood and of great spiritual achievement. Similarly, Martha's conviction of a design in her life served the double purpose of relieving anxiety and of satisfying her dependent needs. It must have sustained her, at times, like the comfort of a friend at her side.

It has often been noted that the individual with a persecution complex may derive much satisfaction from the conclusion that he must have exceptional merits to warrant the efforts made against him. These efforts may suggest that his enemies are jealously resentful of his superiorities.

In every mental hospital there are patients in whom delusions minister to some desire or need that has been denied. Thus, one patient boasts, with sincerity, of his extraordinary inventions, all stolen from him in "thought-form" and patented by others. Another tells of her royal blood, and of the eminent men who have courted her; another talks of a Hollywood mansion she owns, and of the movie star who impatiently awaits her release from the hospital.

Such phenomena of the deluded mind are over-familiar, and the patient who "thinks he's Napoleon" is a hackneyed example of the popular conception of a common type of derangement. Possibly this very familiarity is a reflection of the obvious psychology of such cases, since it is easy to surmise that a frustrated ambition (or "ego") must supply the motive. This much meaning anybody can discover and, moreover, can fully understand. *How* the patient can manage to believe such things may puzzle the layman, but not *why* they are believed, since the need they serve is apparent enough. Often it shows plainly in the bearing and the complacent tone of the patient.

That other needs may support delusional thinking is equally clear. The female patient whose "dream-lover" awaits her release in order to marry her is a familiar figure on the wards. The lover may be a staff member; more often he is someone outside the hospital. He may communicate with the patient by radio or through a television program, conveying messages by way of remarks (sometimes in code or by hint) or gestures in the dialogue. A patient believed me to be in secret liaison with her lover and read between the lines of my comments during therapy sessions what her lover wished to transmit to her. Thus, amorous longings receive some degree of fulfillment and of hope.

The symptoms may thus provide direct satisfaction of the patient's needs, and here the parallel with normal fantasy-making is evident. Imagination, as everyone knows, can provide some very enjoyable substitute satisfactions. For many these may be poor ones, but for those who indulge they are plainly better than nothing. Their obvious shortcoming is, of course, that they are not real. How far more delightful the fantasy if it could be believed in, if the heroic achievement were more than a daydream, the phantom lover a believable reality instead of an acknowledged fiction. It is here that the schizophrenic has his peculiar advantage in the loss or weakening of his perception of reality. Much has been written of his remarkable absorption in his private world. This absorption may seem less remarkable if it is seen as, at least in part, a token that he has made authentic substance out of his dreams.

In summary, then, the symptom has its directly gratifying side, as well as its defensive and expressive aspects. In each respect, moreover, it retains its clear parallel with normal behavior.

can it be a physical disease?

Is this the whole story, or are there different answers to the question: What is schizophrenia? Are there varieties of the disorder, or features of it, that do not fit the anxiety-defense formula?

A quite different view of it has been offered, in language very unlike that of our discussion so far. It considers schizophrenia an illness in the sense of a *disease*, like any other disease, in which certain organs of the body have broken down, or are working poorly. This could result, it has been suggested, from some kind of deteriorative process, or even from an infectious "germ." Discussion of the cause becomes, from this point of view, no longer a matter, fundamentally, of parental personality, emotional and language habits, tendencies toward mis-reading the behavior of others, and so on. It becomes a matter of body pathology, of abnormalities in such organs as the nervous system and the glands, or such processes as the circulation of the blood, energy production and similar vital functions.

A great number of studies have been made of the physical side of schizophrenia. Among the many findings reported may be mentioned low blood pressure, diminished activity of the glands (endocrine), abnormally low consumption of oxygen, abnormal "brain waves."

Some hold the view that the behavior is the consequence of a disorder of the nervous system, with emphasis on the brain. Actual changes in the brain cells of schizophrenics have been reported.

An important finding that has come out of these studies of the body functions is that of diminished activity. The changes in blood circulation, for example, tend to have the character of a *deficiency*. That is, the pressure, the flow and supply of the blood, is *subnormal*. The system is working at a lowered level of operation. There is evidence, moreover, of a tendency for this kind of change to be found in the withdrawn and inactive type of patient, rather than in those who, though perhaps highly delusional, keep up a fair degree of physical and social activity.

That there *are* some abnormal changes among the body processes of some schizophrenics now appears to be fairly generally accepted. As to *how* these changes are related to the behavior described in the preceding pages, two possibilities may be briefly mentioned.

One of these is that the physical disorder causes the symptoms in a way comparable to that in which an invasion of bacteria causes a disease. The disease changes come first, and the behavior changes follow. The frequent withdrawal and apathy, for example, are a reflection of the sluggishness of the physical functions.

Another view reverses this connection. It sees the body changes as symptoms rather than as causes. It proposes that the physical slow-down in the schizophrenic is the effect upon his organic functions of his pulling away from normal stimulation, of the inactivity that results from his apathy about normal pursuits, and of the sedentary life he tends to lead because of his preoccupation with personal problems or with fantasy. The lessened demands he makes on his body cause it to be less responsive. It is as if he were "idling," internally, as a motor idles. It is logical, if he is *living* at a less energetic pace, that his intake of oxygen, for example, would be less, and that his glandular system would be less active.

The withdrawal of the schizophrenic is, of course, emotional as well as physical. To parallel this is evidence that those parts of the nervous system that are basic to the emotional reactions are also functioning in a substandard way. The diminished activity of the glandular system, reported of a great many schizophrenics, has similarly been regarded as the effect of understimulation, in turn seen as the effect of withdrawal and of emotional apathy. The suggested picture is that of an organism which has, in a sense, *relaxed,* or is less alerted, especially in response to stress. What we have here is one more example, perhaps, and among the great variety of examples, in which a way of living— with emphasis on the emotional life—affects the organism, the effect, in brief, of the mind upon the body.

As a demonstration that absence of stimulation may cause organic changes of the type reported in schizophrenia, a study has been cited in which an experimentally blinded animal was found to have atrophied sex glands. This is interpreted to mean that the absence of visual stimulation caused the failure of the gland.

Certainly no observer of the physical stagnation seen on the wards of a mental hospital, of the relative absence of interest in the external world, and of the lack of emotional response, would find it hard to believe that this narrowing and slow-down of the process of living may have a corresponding effect on the organs of the body.

is schizophrenia inherited?

With great frequency the schizophrenic has family members who have been hospitalized for some kind of mental disorder, and sometimes for the same illness. A patient studied by the writer had two schizophrenic brothers, and a sister who was hospitalized for a period with "mental trouble" of undetermined nature. This accounted for four of the five members of the family.

While such a case is exceptional, a major study of over a thousand cases gave evidence of an hereditary factor in this illness. For normal parents the chances are less than one in a hundred that a schizophrenic child will be born. If, however, one parent is schizophrenic, the chances are about sixteen in a hundred that a child will be schizophrenic. If both parents have the disorder, the chances are about two out of three that a child will have it. If one of a pair of identical twins is schizophrenic, the chances are better than four out of five that the other will be so. But if the factor of biological heredity is smaller, as in fraternal (or ordinary) twins, the chances of the illness in the twin of a schizophrenic are only about one in seven.

There are cases in which the hereditary factor is regarded as showing itself with particular clearness. These cases exhibit features rather different from those described in this book.

It is often difficult to set a time when the illness begins. This is because the person is commonly described as having always been different or peculiar, so that the symptoms, when they first appear, seem to have developed gradually out of what were earlier simply traits of personality. The difficulty of finding a beginning is increased by the common absence of any discoverable stress experience.

In the reports of such cases there is, again, an emphasis on unusual social behavior. The child is "a bit odd." He keeps much to himself. If there is a neighborhood group, he tends to be

on the fringe, rather than a participating member. He is an on-
looker, aloof, diffident. His interests tend to be solitary, though
he is often very close to his mother. He has no close friends of his
own age, and often does not seem to want any. He rarely takes
the initiative in a conversation. He is uncomfortable when people call at home. He rarely confides, tends to keep his feelings to
himself.

A patient said, in talking of his boyhood:

> I know now that there was something wrong, but I didn't
> see it then. The boys around my age in our neighborhood
> spent most of their time together, but I was never included.
> I don't believe I thought about it much. I guess I just took
> it for granted. I know I was shy. I remember that I couldn't
> seem to understand those boys. They'd make remarks to me
> and I couldn't seem to get what they meant. I mean it seemed
> like it was something they all understood but I didn't because
> I was an outsider. Sometimes I would try to "break in," but
> they never treated me like they did each other. They would
> look at me in a different way, that made me feel I was funny
> or queer. They would say things to each other and look at
> me and laugh. So usually I kept to myself. There was another
> boy I used to spend some time with, but he was more like
> me. He was quiet and shy. He didn't belong to the group
> either.

A frequent finding in cases of early and gradual onset is a
lack of interest in activities in which most children show some
degree of zest. The boy seems content to do nothing, much of the
time. He is colorless, lacks spontaneity, has no enthusiasms. Despite the apparent apathy and dullness there may, however, be
evidence of sensitivity.

The patient may be hospitalized, finally, because his
peculiarities reach a degree that forces the family to seek medical
advice. Or some feature of his behavior develops into a fairly
specific *symptom*. For example, a tendency toward irritability or
temper tantrums may finally culminate in a potentially dangerous
threat, or a hostile act toward a parent. Or a tendency toward

suspiciousness finally becomes a charge that others are annoying or behaving in some unfriendly way.

If there is an hereditary factor in schizophrenia, what does it mean in terms of the kind of experiences and the kind of anxieties and hostilities illustrated in the studies surveyed? Can such cases as the type just described—sometimes referred to as "constitutional"—be fitted to the ideas outlined in this chapter?

It is important to emphasize at the outset that regardless of the evidence of an hereditary factor *there is a correspondence*, in our cases, between an experience and the symptom. Marcella's delusions "corresponded" to the painful episodes of her girlhood. Another girl might not have developed from such episodes so painful or so lasting a complex, perhaps, so we may have to allow that Marcella was "different" in this respect. But she not only *had* such a complex; she had also experienced depreciation as a child. There is no reason to suppose she would have been the same had she been praised and felt accepted.

Similarly there can be no reason to doubt that the link between Florrie's "voices" and the fact that she had engaged in forbidden sex behavior, or between Marilyn's puzzled impressions of competing forces in the world about her, and her conflicting feelings toward her husband. *Something happened to these people*, in each case, *that showed a clear connection with the kind of disorder they developed*. The best evidence, in fact, that schizophrenia is related to the events of life is provided, as many observers have noted, by cases in which heavy stresses, bearing upon a non-schizoid person, result in an illness from which recovery is rapid when the stress is removed.

There does remain a question, however, whether the experiences to which these disorders were traced are to be seen as *entirely* responsible for them. With great frequency it seems very safe to say that the crucial experience is too common among *non*-schizophrenics to supply the whole or what is needed for an answer. *Why* do certain persons react in this exceptional way to the ordinary stresses of life?

It is here that the idea of a predisposing factor comes into focus. Two answers have been given. According to one, this factor introduces something new and different, something foreign and not yet fully defined, a "mysterious intruder" among the traits and responses so far described in our cases. Whatever this peculiar "something" is, it is often referred to as a mental process not easily understandable in terms of anything that goes on in the minds of normal people.

The second possibility is that schizophrenia is simply a label for what happens to certain persons through an unfortunate combination of circumstances and personality. It is the outcome of particular early experiences and a particular kind of emotional disposition or temperament. It results mainly from the impact of parental treatment upon a child who, among other things, reacts—more than most children—sensitively and painfully to rejection, who lacks normal ability to tolerate this kind of pain (perhaps other kinds as well), and whose persistence in the effort to adjust to other people is small.

This "certain kind of person" is to be seen, in other words, in terms of extremes of normal behavior traits. If it is "natural" for a child to experience anxiety when threatened, it may be equally "natural" for some children to react with a greater amount of anxiety to the *same* degree of threat. The consequence of this will be a more vivid, more sharply distressing emotion, more lasting in its effects. So far as this anxiety is most vitally linked with the sense of personal worth and adequacy, it will be in a setting of tests and challenges of this kind that the individual will be most highly sensitized and suffer his greatest distresses.

If, further, most of us feel a degree of resentment under disrespect or scorn, some may react to it much beyond the ordinary. If certain nervous systems react with exceptional readiness and intensity to such stimuli, the occasional marked prominence of hostile behavior, and likewise its persistence, would be expected. The schizophrenic whose sustained resentfulness and bitterness makes him conspicuous is a familiar figure in many hospitals. One may not find evidence, however, in the life history of such a patient, of provocations which appear to be correspondingly exceptional.

All of us, again, suffer frustration when the effort to prove our adequacy and establish our worth fails. To get a low mark, to lose a contest, to seek praise and be denied it, to bid for recognition and meet refusal, all these mean unhappy moments for anyone. Yet it seems just as safe to believe that people may differ, apart from experiences, with respect to *how much* they suffer this kind of unpleasantness, as it is safe to believe they differ in every other way. There is no need to think that everybody's sensibilities are exactly the same. For all we know to the contrary, some people may be "born oversensitive."

If this were true we should expect that such a person would not endure disappointments as well as others. Failures and frustrations being more painful, he would stop trying sooner, and he would tend to avoid situations in which these painful experiences might occur. Some allowance may also be made for the possibility that his ability to persist, his stamina, might be less than that of others. Often descriptions of the behavior of a child that exhibits schizoid traits suggest that, among other things, his *drives* tend to be weak, his interest in the world about him less than average.

It may be that sensitivity beyond the normal is related, not only to the withdrawal tendency, but to the exceptionally prolonged emotional effects of early experiences, as illustrated in several of our cases. All of us outgrow many emotional wounds of childhood. If, in some, the effects of these wounds appear to persist remarkably into adult life, it may be in part because the original experience was a more vivid and painful one. The often-noted immaturity of the schizophrenic, linked, as earlier suggested, to anxiety, may thus be understood as rooted to a degree of sensitivity that checks his growth impulses.

For all the consequences of the frustration of whatever impulse the budding schizophrenic might have toward contacts with people and things, he would retain essentially normal needs, and these would often tend to express in fantasies, and in the building up of a private world to replace the one renounced. By further advances in such an in-grown mode of living, equally private ways of thinking and even of language usage might be expected to develop.

A frequent observation of those who have spent much time with the schizophrenic is the difficulty of getting close to him. Despite one's best efforts to break through his aloofness, to get in tune, there often remains a distance, a reserve, a marked lack of warmth in his responses. This failure to feel that one has truly made contact has led many to the belief that the schizophrenic has lost, or at any rate lacks, the ability for a certain kind of relationship with others.

This relationship depends on the ability to *enter, emotionally,* into the emotional life of another. It is the ability to understand the feelings of another by feeling one's self as he feels. It is illustrated in the experiences we may express when we say, "I am strongly in sympathy with his feelings in the matter."

How could a lack of "feeling ability" come about? It seems possible that it might result from chronic anxiety concerning one's acceptance by others. A person constantly preoccupied with *himself,* and with the attitudes of others toward himself, might fail to develop this kind of feeling. To participate in the feelings of another, to project one's self into that person's emotional life, one must *forget one's self,* at least for a time. The schizophrenic may be too self-centered to do this, too occupied with his own doubts and fears about himself.

But there may be another source of such a lack. The basic capacity for *learning* to co-experience emotions in this way may vary from person to person as all human capacities vary. If this were true, certain features of delusions, for example, might be more easily understood, such as the fact that they so often suggest a remarkable defect in knowledge of human feelings, and especially human motives. The ability to comprehend the way others feel in terms of one's own emotional life may contribute importantly to the accurate thinking about behavior which so often seems lacking in the development of delusions.

This view of schizophrenia regards it, then, as the result of a particular pattern of variations of normal human traits and tendencies. A "particular pattern" does not, of course, mean anything like a fixed combination. The cases used in our survey show how great the differences may be from patient to patient. The idea that schizophrenia is related to sensitivity about personal acceptance, to anxiety about it, to resentment when denied it, to weakness of confidence, to low tolerance for distress, to poor comprehension of emotional states, poor grasp of reality, etc., leaves plenty of room for differences in the number and the degree of these traits present, as well as in other features of personality.

More important than this, however, is the possibility that the "predisposition" to schizophrenia is no more than this patterning of traits, and that the disorder develops when a person with a few or many of them encounters a particular sequence of experiences. From this point of view, cases of the early development of the disorder may be seen as the effect of the presence, in extraordinary degree, of the factors that make people vulnerable. When sensitivity reaches the point at which a *normal* amount of threat is overwhelming, the effect on behavior might very well suggest a disorder arising wholly from within.

11. what can

be done?

The view of the emotional basis of schizophrenia presented in the preceding pages leads fairly directly to certain conclusions as to what may be done to assist the stricken person toward recovery. The problems of treatment are closely related to the basic sources of the disorder. Since this interpretation of schizophrenia has been psychological, it follows that we will here be concerned mainly with the psychological approach to therapy.

On the surface, at least, the task of therapy does not look too difficult. If Florrie's "voices" arose from sex guilt, why not help her to condemn her guilt a little less harshly? Without any aim to "loosen" her morals, a more tolerant attitude toward her weakness, which would enable her to accept herself more fully, might be suggested. It might also be explained to her why, through excessive anxiety about social acceptance, she suffered so acutely over her transgressions. Finally, the meaning of the voices themselves might be offered.

If, again, Marcella's trouble was rooted in strong feelings of rejection and a resulting strong habit of misinterpreting what she saw and heard, why not simply make all this clear to her, and therefore enable her to understand the source of all her difficulties with people? If she is fairly intelligent, and willing to discuss the possible role of a personal factor in her problem, why not trace her inadequacy feeling to its sources for her, and show how it led her to make errors in perceiving what she saw and heard until she had developed a full-blown persecution complex?

the emotional relationship as therapy

While, in the individual case, and with certain factors favorable, such procedures may meet with some success, with others the problem is far from simple. For one thing, the therapist himself may be included in the illness, as it were. He may not be accepted as a helper at all. In keeping with the patient's attitude toward people in general, the therapist may be seen as threatening, rejecting, untrustworthy. He may be fitted into the delusional system as "just another persecutor." He may become an object of the hostility which the patient feels, compulsively, toward anyone regarded as superior in role. Or the patient with a lifelong habit of keeping personal problems shut tightly within, may be unwilling or even unable to reveal himself. His reactions may continue to be strongly marked by the guardedness, the distance and the tendency to withdraw that have habitually characterized his attitude toward people. If for years he has been convinced that others quite commonly doubt his worth, it is likely that this conviction will express itself to some degree in his emotional reactions to the therapist.

In short, the patient very often directly shows, during his conversations with the therapist, some of the symptoms of his social and emotional disorder. What happened to him originally through experiences with his parents or with parent figures, often now colors his perceptions of each new person on the social horizon.

Yet, if it is true that this illness grows out of what may be termed a failure in normal emotional relationships with others, it follows that there should also be a certain kind of relationship with another person which can be used helpfully to overcome this failure. If, in brief, one kind of experience with a person or persons has led to unhealthy social tendencies, it should be possible for a new and different kind of experience with some person (that is, with the therapist) to modify these tendencies in a healthier direction.

Whether this task will be fairly easy or very difficult will depend significantly on certain characteristics of the individual patient. If he is delusional, and if his delusions give him a great deal of satisfaction, it may be with extreme difficulty that he can be persuaded to abandon them. This will be especially true if giving them up would not only deprive him of gratification of certain needs, but force him to face some painful realities about himself. It may be, too, that the conflict basic to the disorder is so agonizing to the self-esteem, or so intensely charged with guilt or remorse, that the patient, unhappy though he may be, cannot be brought to confront it. He may even accept the wisdom of a frank review of the "emotional jam" that brought him to the hospital, yet find himself unable, because of the strength of his feelings, to open up the conflict areas to discussion. His attitude may mean, in effect: "It's too painful. I just can't talk about it."

To penetrate this barrier becomes the first task of treatment. The therapist must begin the process of normalizing the patient's social self, not by way of a "technique," but by offering him the *acceptance,* the *respect* and the *tolerance* which may be regarded as the elements of a good human relationship, regardless of setting or purpose. Such treatment often amounts to a reversal of what has happened to the patient to make him what he is. If the stress laid in Chapter 10 upon the importance of early experiences was justified, we may say that treatment must be "counter-parental" in quality. Sympathetic acceptance of the patient by the therapist must, moreover, be *genuine.* The patient cannot be deceived for long. There are those who would advise, in fact: "If you find that you cannot really *like* your patient, send him to someone who can, for you are sure to fail in your effort to help him."

Such an attitude will help to achieve the patience and the carefulness that will often be needed. The sensitivity of the schizophrenic, the occasional exaggerated touchiness of his pride, are familiar to all who have worked with him. His responsiveness to anything that can possibly be interpreted as rejection is remarkable. When a patient suddenly became silent during an interview with me, it was revealed that she had taken a slight frown (possibly an unconscious mark of momentary perplexity on my part) to mean disapproval of her. Another froze in anger when I spoke a few words in greeting to another patient passing by; she felt the visiting period to be exclusively her own and resented the intrusion of anyone else upon it, however briefly. A third tore her dress to pieces when I was forced to keep her waiting too long in my office after an interruption. She explained later that every added minute of waiting showed how much less important I considered her than someone else, and she became overwhelmed with resentful anger.

One who likes schizophrenics will, therefore, have an advantage in treating them. His spontaneous expressions of this liking will immediately be felt by the patient. When it is, and when along with this liking there is respect for the human personality in all of its manifestations, a genuine interest in the essential problem of the schizophrenic and a desire to help him with it, the therapeutic task will be well begun.

The therapist must also impress with his tolerance. The patient must be sure that whatever he reveals in the way of thoughts or impulses he thinks are discreditable will be received and accepted only as a part of the problem. He must know that the therapist will continue to accept and respect him and will continue to want to help him as a *person*, regardless of the fact that what he acknowledges may not always be admirable. He must know that his hostilities, his jealousies, his fears and his "guilty desires" are here viewed—as perhaps nowhere else—as natural phenomena, to be understood and not judged in the usual moral sense.

The importance of the emotional relationship can hardly be exaggerated. There are those who believe that much improvement in the patient results from this factor alone, and that sometimes the therapist himself may be deceived in thinking that it is the effectiveness of the rational appeals he has made that have brought recovery, when in reality the vital fact may be that, by fully accepting the patient, he has enabled him to accept himself. It seems agreed among many who have worked with the schizophrenic that if he is finally to be brought back to reality he must first of all be brought back into at least one wholehearted and healthy human relationship through the *personal* influence of the therapist.

Being quite human himself, the latter's own personality traits may at times be important. The effect may be favorable or unfavorable. If he was once inclined to be a somewhat shy and diffident person himself, he may have more patience with the schizophrenic whose shyness and diffidence are of extreme degree. He will also understand better the skills needed to overcome this barrier. If he has, on the other hand, a tendency toward anxiety, or feels insecure in his own social relationships, he may feel disturbingly threatened when confronted with the hostility so often displayed by the schizophrenic. Some patients are, in fact, quite adept at "getting under the skin" of the therapist, and may genuinely test his control.

So far as the patient's emotional disorder consists at its roots of a transfer to others of his habitual reactions to his parents, the main task of the therapist is to provide the patient with an emotional experience with *another* close and very important person. So far as the patient's dependent needs are satisfied, his relationship with the therapist may even be seen as, to a degree, the same as that with his father.

It is in the *differences* that the real importance lies. It is a new kind of social experience. It is intended as a correction for the old one. If the latter caused the patient to begin the withdrawal from humanity in anxious distrust, the new one, in therapy, must help him to want to return to it. It is through the personality of the therapist, with his acceptance, his tolerance and his fairness that the patient is encouraged to re-open himself to emotional contacts and relationships with others. In this sense, therapy may be a kind of spiritual restoration. It has even been seen as having, at its best, some resemblance to a religious "conversion," at least so far as the quality of its feeling is concerned. The patient is being helped to return to his fellow man, renouncing his isolation and his suspicion.

This, to be sure, is a large order, and doubtless a great amount of therapy falls short to some degree of so ideal a goal. A relationship in which the patient feels that the therapist can at all times be trusted to be truthful and reasonable is enough, however, to provide a foundation for much progress.

A patient exhibited, from time to time, marked hostility toward me. This was always traceable to a mis-reading of various facial expressions, gestures or remarks. Invariably the patient saw rejection in these bits of behavior. Behind these errors lay his strongly habitual tendency to feel himself unfavorably regarded by others. Quick anger followed each impression of rejection. Despite an excellent relationship, these spells occurred in an automatic and seemingly compulsive manner.

He was assured, after each of these episodes, that his impressions were wrong. It is highly doubtful that this alone would have had any lasting effect. Far more important was the repeated experience, hour after hour and week after week, of a secure emotional relationship. The goodwill was there, sincere and unmistakable. At last it registered. He was able, finally, to *feel* the truth. The meaning of the sharp contradiction between this well-grounded conviction of acceptance in the therapy relationship, and the momentary and jarring impressions of disapproval, was finally clear. Once *doubt* of such impressions was lodged in this way, it was possible to undermine more extensive delusional interpretations. This doubt could not have been implanted by logical appeals. Only the newly established habit of *feeling* could displace it.

The basis of delusional thinking is often highly visible in the patient's behavior. The distrust, for example, the feeling of rejection and the resulting hostility, may show with considerable intensity. These may be the feelings, still active, from which the symptom originally grew. The emotional roots of the disorder are directly on display. It is, as earlier suggested, through the emotional factor in the therapy itself that they are most effectively dislodged.

A schizophrenic boy left my office at the end of an interview. He returned almost immediately, much disturbed. His face showed hostility, but also bewilderment. He said he had heard me remark: "I'm always glad to see him go. He makes me sick." This kind of hallucinated rejection had characterized the patient's illness for some time.

The incident temporarily shattered the previous good feeling. While the hostility did not last, there was coolness and reserve, a marked increase in distance. Every attempt was made to point out how altogether without motive or reason such a remark by the writer would have been. Gradually the good feeling was restored. Weeks later the incident was referred to in connection with a discussion of the effect of reasoning on delusional beliefs and of "voices." The boy then said, with some embarrassment and considerable hesitation: "It wasn't what you said that convinced me that what I heard was not you. It was the day you invited me to go to the commissary with you for coffee. It was your lunch hour and I knew you were off duty. So I felt you must really want me to come." This casual token of friendliness had outweighed, for the patient, all the reasons he could be given.

The best therapeutic relationship is often described as that in which the therapist assumes the role of a *good* father toward the patient. This emphasis means that the therapist must behave, to the best of his ability, as a kind of model parent, or at least as a type of parent-figure that is new and usually very unlike the patient's own parents. The ideal parent provides, of course, emotional support when needed for his child's morale. Beyond this, however, he recognizes that he must not only aid but must allow his child to grow in independence and in initiative. If he is too demanding and too strongly supportive, the child will be weakened and will fail to develop self-reliance. In a similar role the therapist must remember that eventually the patient must be enabled to function on his own.

On the whole, the comparison of the therapist's role with that of the good father is helpful in making clear that his work is in part designed to correct the persisting effects of the original parental treatment. In reality, much of this work could as well be described in terms of what is ordinarily meant by a friendship. The good friend, like the good father, is devoted in the sense that he does not judge, or condemn, nor does he try to control. He can be firm at need. He may not always approve us, yet we think of him as always on our side.

Many believe, as mentioned before, that the emotional relationship may bring gains which the therapist himself ascribes to techniques which he thinks of as the truly essential part of his tools of treatment. It may also happen that something the therapist may regard as incidental turns out to be very influential. I was once told by a patient who was about to be discharged from the hospital that what she would remember longer than any of her discussions with me had happened quite accidentally. An interview had been interrupted by a paranoid patient in a very hostile state who heatedly denounced me. A few quiet words properly suited to the nature of the patient's disturbance were all that were needed to subdue him. The first patient, who had observed this, said: "I admired your self-control so much I decided that for my main goal I would learn to think about people in the way that kept you from getting upset." Actually, the handling of the incident had been routine, and hardly to be regarded as self-control. For the patient, however, it had the value, apparently, of a concrete and vivid example, compared with what for her had been, perhaps, "mere talk" about human relationships.

In another instance a patient said his morale had been lifted, more than by anything else, by my casual confession that I was a bit depressed by what I felt was an avoidable error I had made in dealing with another case. The patient said: "I had sort of idealized you a bit. So I thought if *you* could pull a boner and let it get you down, I figured it could happen to anybody and I wasn't so stupid after all."

self-understanding as therapy

Our description of the experiences of the mentally ill began with the account of Florrie and the voices. What brought her to the hospital, it will be recalled, were the emotional upsets that resulted from these experiences. So long as she continued to believe in their reality, she exhibited disturbed behavior. The first step in laying a foundation for therapy was, in this case, to develop some doubt that people were really talking about her. The achievement of this step was much aided by the building up, over a period of several weeks, of a bond of trust in the therapist. To a degree, Florrie was able to accept, on faith, that the voices were a symptom of disorder.

Yet this was obviously not enough. For one thing, the faith rested largely on Florrie's feeling toward the therapist. This in turn was kept alive by frequent supportive interviews. If she were ever to leave the hospital, it would have to be replaced by something more permanent. She must be provided with an answer to the question: If people aren't actually talking, where do the voices come from? If they aren't what I think they are, then what *are* they?

The next step in treatment, then, is to make clear the *meaning* of the behavior that makes up the symptoms. To this must be added, so far as this meaning is understood by the therapist, and so far as it is possible to explain it to the patient.

In Florrie's case this was not difficult to do. It meant, first of all, to help her to stand off from herself a bit and to view her personality as if a part of her were to become, for a while, a mere observer. (To assist with this, among other devices, she was allowed to read certain selections from her own case history.) Florrie had been pretty closely wrapped up within herself. She needed to see herself a little more "from the outside"; that is, as others might see her. To make clear the background of her adult personality, some of her childhood experiences were reviewed. The ways in which a person's conscience grows through parental exhortation and taboos, through rewards and punishments, were outlined. That she was not "born with a conscience" was stressed. The personality-picture of Florrie's mother was revived and considered. This was not to judge or to blame, but to appraise her influence on Florrie's development, and especially upon her sense of right and wrong. Her emotional relationship with her mother was discussed as thoroughly as her recollections would permit.

Finally, the meaning of the "voices" was presented in a way somewhat similar to that outlined in Chapter 1. The fact that the charges she "heard" were the same as her own self-judgments before her illness began was pointed out. She was reminded that not only did *what* the voices say sound like a conscience, but even the way they said it at times (that is, in a whisper), was the way a conscience was supposed to talk. Simple illustrations of the way in which the mind might work to create such experiences were offered, such as a comparison with a public address system by which the voice of a person speaking might easily be made to appear to come from various locations.

A hint, at least, as to the underlying purpose of this remarkable displacement of conscience from its usual channels of expression was given. Following this, an effort was made to soften, to some degree, the moral judgment Florrie had made upon herself. Without seeking to alter her sexual ethics in any essential way, a less rigid and less harsh point of view was indicated. In consideration of the sincerity of her penitence, a more forgiving attitude toward her error was suggested. She was encouraged, in other words, to accept herself despite her failings, and to see herself as, if no better, at least no worse than a great many other "sinners."

When delusions not only defend against anxiety but provide gratifications as well, they may be very difficult to dislodge. Also difficult to treat are the people whose perceptions are chronically distorted by hostility. In her calmer moods Marcella, for example, seemed at times on the brink of realization of the way in which her highly sensitized complex, rooted in the painful experience of childhood, had colored and twisted her relationships with others. There were moments when she seemed to glimpse what it was that had caused her to feel a social outcast in a world that in reality was as friendly toward her as toward anyone else.

At mention of her neighbors, however, the calm quickly vanished. Her tone changed, her eyes hardened, and the bitterness returned as she reviewed their abuses and their hostile acts. Resentment overwhelmed her. Not only was all reasonableness swept away, but even the *impulse* to achieve it as well. At these times Marcella was like the patient who could say of her estranged husband: "I don't *want* to be 'fair' to him; I hate him too much."

Where hostility is not so sustained, and especially in the early stages of delusional thinking, the possibilities of successful treatment become much greater. They rest at the outset heavily on some degree of realization by the patient that *something is wrong*, that his life is not what it could be. The therapist may put the critical question thus: "Granted that you feel very sure of these ideas, and that you sincerely believe that you have reasons enough for feeling sure, are you willing, nevertheless, to at least discuss, to review and re-examine some of these reasons?" A "yes" answer to this, even a grudging one, is a definite sign of hope.

In treatment of the delusional patient, incidents of contemporary behavior may be helpful. Direct misinterpretations of the therapist's own behavior may, as earlier indicated, be spotted, brought into focus, and examined. Such "garden varieties" of delusion may then be held up as specimens of what may become something larger and more dangerous. When Marcella, for example, expressed her feeling that she was to be transferred to another hospital because of a remark she had overheard that suggested to her that she had been found unwanted, she could be told, in effect, "This is *it*. Here is an excellent specimen of what has brought you here. Now let's examine it carefully." Once such errors can be directly shown, the way is clear for a progressive undermining of the symptom.

The patient may be encouraged to bring similar incidents from his day-to-day experiences in contacts with other patients. A remark at which he took offense, or in which he found a slight, may be studied with the therapist. Sometimes the other person involved may be brought in for such discussions. Concrete samples of this kind may provide starting points for reviews of the past, or as present proofs of probable errors of the past.

What is the value of explaining the symptom to the patient?

By explaining it, it is given a new and different meaning. By changing its meaning, its emotional effect is altered.

Such changes in meaning are a familiar part of everyday experience. An acquaintance returns our greeting with a cool and abstracted air. We feel rebuffed and a bit resentful. Later we learn, perhaps, that he had been preoccupied and distraught over some bad news. Our feeling toward his behavior is immediately reversed, because its meaning has been altered.

A young girl, mentioned earlier, experienced a sexual threat during interviews with me. The experience was convincingly traced to an erotic advance, many years before, by an uncle. The role of past events in present emotional reactions was explained to her, and the irrational and compulsive character of her anxiety was made clear. Following this, while the thought, and the feelings of anticipation of a sexual advance did recur, the anxiety it had occasioned was much reduced. What had been felt as a real threat was now recognized as only a symptom. ("I see now that it isn't really you; it's me.")

A patient was disturbed by the feeling that her thoughts were being read. She noticed this particularly when in contact with people who represented authority, such as supervisors and employers. The experience was traced to a childhood incident in which it had seemed to her that her domineering mother was somehow able to know what was going on in her mind. Her mother had, in fact, at times hinted that this was true. The patient was able to accept this interpretation; that is, she found it plausible and convincing. While the reaction was not abolished as a result of this understanding, it was no longer so disturbing.

It no longer meant telepathy. It meant, simply, that a painful part of her past was still alive.

While the giving of insight into the meaning of the symptom is considered by some a basic essential of treatment, other features of the therapy relationship must also be emphasized. The patient often needs a reawakening of interest in face-to-face human contacts. To encourage the "back to reality" movement he needs to learn how enjoyable people may be when he can meet them with enough confidence to feel that he is handling his end with skill, or at least with adequacy. He may find, when sufficiently encouraged, that he can express himself better than he supposed, and that expressing himself improves his ability to do it and increases his pleasure in it.

With regard to social confidence, the patient's morale can be raised in a variety of direct and indirect ways. The positive achievements of his life, however modest, may be reviewed as tokens of his potential. His assets may be detailed for him, and their reality stressed. The therapist, by listening attentively to what the patient has to say, is assuring him that he is worth listening to. If the therapist, moreover, for his part views the human problems he faces as worthy of his deepest professional interest, his attentive listening can be altogether sincere. He will ask the patient's opinions, and will treat them, when he gets them, as worth the asking. He will quote the patient, or recall things he has said, to show that they were worth remembering. He can, in asking for decisions, convey confidence that the patient can make them. He can convey, too, a hint that, right or wrong, the patient's *own* decisions will do him in the long run more good than those of anyone else.

When, along with corrected social perception, a restored interest in, and attitude toward, social experience reaches the stage where it can be *transferred* from the therapist to other people, the main substance of the task of treatment will be on the way to achievement. In broadest terms it may be said that while the disorder itself represents a transfer to others of the effects of earlier experiences, successful therapy may be seen as a further transfer, again to others, of the self-understanding and social confidence gained in therapy.

This book is an effort to set forth the psychological interpretation of schizophrenic disorders. Discussion in this chapter deals mainly, therefore, with the corresponding method of treatment. A brief word may be included, however, concerning the very widely used chemical and electrical methods of therapy, that is, the convulsive or shock treatments.

That such treatment leads to improvement, to some degree and in some cases, seems to be fairly generally accepted. The interpretation of how this improvement comes about is in a very unsettled state.

Some regard shock as little more than an occasional aid to psychotherapy, on the ground that, in one way or another, it causes the patient to become more open to the effort to reach him, psychologically. Others regard it as effective in itself, and as therefore often worth trying with patients who fail to respond to psychological efforts, or with those who, because there aren't enough therapists, cannot be given this kind of treatment.

There are grounds for the view that improvement resulting from shock represents treatment of the symptom rather than of the cause. One way of thinking of this is that such treatment simply blocks off the emotional problem by "knocking out" the part of the nervous system that corresponds to it. Like giving a sedative for pain, this relieves the patient of the distressing effects of his trouble without getting at its roots. Many medical treatments are of this character, of course, and their usefulness is fully accepted.

This interpretation of the effects of shock treatment is clearly in line with the view of schizophrenia presented in this book. That such treatment may remove the elements of an emotional conflict or problem (on the analogy of a memory loss, perhaps) seems understandable. It is equally clear that it cannot, in itself, solve the problem. It cannot change the personality in a constructive way, nor can it restore morale in the way it is restored by experiences of acceptance and of achievement.

As would be expected in the treatment of a developmental disorder in this way, the favorable effects are very often temporary. When shock is induced by the injection of insulin, for example, the improvement may be less lasting even than that in patients who improve without such treatment. Basic emotional habits, often dating from early childhood, are not so altered, and when the improved patient is returned, as he often is, to a life situation which is the same or very similar to the one in which he became ill, a relapse very often follows.

how can it be prevented?

Once well begun, and especially when fully established, the schizophrenic disorders may be difficult to treat. A logical question therefore concerns the possibility of prevention. Can the budding schizophrenic child be recognized, for example, and how can the tendency be checked?

Among the reports of early schizophrenia is one in which a relationship between the behavior of the child and personality of the parents is clearly evident. This study of fifty-five children indicated that the disorder may be recognized during the first two years of life, and may be apparent as early as the second half-year. It is seen in marked withdrawal from contact with people, and in a sharply contrasting interest in all kinds of *things*. The child's use of language, moreover, is more an expression of his own preoccupation than of a desire to communicate his thoughts to others.

In the descriptive accounts given, the child seems hardly aware of the presence of people, or he tends to accept their presence in a perfunctory way. He may answer a question rarely, and may seldom speak to anyone spontaneously. He often appears irritated by the intrusion of others upon his absorption with his thoughts, or upon his play with toys or other objects. His tendency to shut out *people* may be illustrated when he is checked from a movement, for example. He reacts to the obstructing *hand* alone, as if it were detached from the person.

Such a child may be so little responsive to others as to be mistaken for a mental defective, or as deaf. Yet his expression may be thoughtful, his memory excellent, his intelligence beyond question.

The parents of the children studied were conspicuously intelligent and included many members of the professional classes. They were successful and sophisticated people. None of the children had had any disease or injury to which the disorder could be traced.

It was found that the parents could be clearly characterized as cool, distant and impersonal toward their children. Treatment of the child, although adequate in relation to its physical needs and well-being, tended to be mechanical and perfunctory. The mothers were often lacking in any affectional warmth. They might be quite attentive to the child, proud of its achievements, concerned about its obedience and good habits; they might, in fact, really want to do a good job as parents. Yet they consistently treated the child without genuine feeling and without real enjoyment.

The investigator states: "I saw only one mother (of such a child) who proceeded to embrace him warmly and bring her face close to his." Some of the fathers, it seemed, hardly knew their children. In an effort to arouse one of these detached fathers —or to see if he *was* arousable—he was asked if he thought he would recognize his children if he saw them in the street. Far from becoming resentful, the father replied, after reflection, that he was not sure that he would!

Many of these parents said they were not comfortable with people, and described themselves as undemonstrative. The marriages tended to be rather cold and formal. There was little evidence that these people had been strongly attracted to each other, or that they were capable of being impetuous. The reported fact that there had been only one divorce in the fifty-five marriages is suggestive, not so much of good marital adjustment as of a lack of the intensity of emotion necessary to such a breach. To some degree, perhaps, the partners reacted to their mates with as little feeling as they did to their children. The fathers were, as a group, engrossed in their work, and had themselves been sternly reared in emotional refrigerators.

While the study does not supply evidence of the possible basis of the emotional condition of these children in terms of maternal behavior (for example, the character of mothering treatment, or its relative absence), it is not difficult to picture the effect of such domestic atmospheres. The fact that, while unresponsive to persons, *things* greatly attracted these children, is suggestive, at least, that there may have been a decided difference in the receptivity of these two kinds of "objects" which led to the avoidance of, or indifference to, one of them. The fact that the children did not apparently accept their parents even *as objects* gives a hint that some degree of initial interest either failed to reward or led to rebuff.

Yet this is not the whole story.* Among the children of these same parents were some who did *not* exhibit such behavior. Parents of this type may, in fact, have children who, far from showing avoidance behavior, may even be markedly aggressive. One student reports the repeated finding of "schizophrenic children whose mothers appear not to lack warmth, genuine love or acceptance . . ."

Can sense be made of such apparent contradictions?

The findings suggest that children differ in basic emotional temperament. They suggest that some are more sensitive than others, and that some have more drive and will be, under rebuff, more persistent and aggressive than others.

It was earlier proposed that if a child's original sensitivity is

---

* A different category of childhood disorder has been described by Mahler, in which, in contrast with the type here discussed, the child's relationship to its mother is extremely close; so much so, in fact, that when the process of psychological weaning begins, the child is overwhelmed by separation anxiety. His panic is so great that delusions and hallucinations develop to restore the intimate fusion with the mother image.

extreme enough, or if the forward thrust of his social motive is weak enough, he may tend to withdraw even under the normal frustrations and denials that a child must encounter with normally responsive parents. Among the fifty children Kanner studied there must have been many degrees of such sensitivity, many degrees of need of response from parents, and many degrees of persistence and stamina in the face of indifference. Some of these children would have perhaps become schizophrenic even in a "warm" environment. The important point to stress is that some of them might *not* have done so, and that it may not have been, in a few or in many instances, an accident that a withdrawn child was found to have indifferent or repelling parents.

The term "schizoid" has sometimes been applied to the shy and inactive child who exhibits an inclination to withdraw. Can withdrawal in childhood be used as a warning marker of a tendency toward a schizophrenic development, and therefore as an indicator of the need of treatment to check the onset of the illness?

It has emphatically not been shown, as indicated in the preceding chapter, that all withdrawn children become schizophrenic. Several studies have failed to supply such proof. Some schizophrenics, moreover, have apparently been normally sociable as children. One study showed, for example, that only about one out of five of a large number of hospitalized schizophrenics had been withdrawn from childhood.

A tendency to withdraw, taken simply as a trait of behavior, may have various meanings. A boy who avoids rough play because he is physically unable to cope with it can hardly be said to have an unhealthy social attitude. A boy who withdraws from social activities because of his strong interest in books, or in his stamp collection, or in building model airplanes, is certainly not to be regarded as in need of psychiatric attention. The only kind of seclusiveness or solitariness which need concern a parent, as one mental hygienist points out, is that prompted by feelings of self-depreciation.[1] It is when a boy withdraws, not so much through *attraction* to solitary interests, as because he feels that he is not liked, or that he would be rejected if some weakness (for example, his masturbation or his cowardice) were known to others, that his withdrawal may be seen as unfavorable in meaning.

Students of mental health have stressed, however, that unnecessary anxiety may be aroused in parents by the attachment of sinister meanings to every variety of unusual behavior. A preventive policy "does not call for the indiscriminate curbing of every mode of childish behavior which bears a resemblance to some symptom of psychotic behavior in the adult." [2]

It should not, however, be difficult to recognize the progressive *desocialization* which reflects failure to gain satisfying responses from others. In the history of a group of schizophrenics who had formerly been normally sociable a sequence of stages was noted. In the beginning, efforts to gain companionship were exhibited. These efforts continued despite experiences of exclusion. Finally, social failure was accepted, and interests were shifted. The effect of this defeatism on behavior then made the individual less acceptable to others. This, in turn, led to further exclusions.

The last stage is often clearly indicated when a boy becomes marked for shyness or aloofness. Not only is he likely to be accepted in his self-adopted role of outsider. He may become a butt of ridicule and other more active forms of rejection.

The conclusion to be drawn from the foregoing discussion seems clear enough. When the motive for withdrawal is uncertainty or anxiety about dislike or disapproval, and when the tendency to recede is fairly consistently shown rather than occasional, it may be seen as at least worthy of concern. While it cannot, on the basis of present evidence, be regarded as schizoid in the sense of foreshadowing either mental disorder or even a seclusive personality, it may be viewed as a possible threat to future social relationships. While the boy may not become a schizophrenic or even a recluse (though he *could* become either) it is quite certain that he is having some unhappy moments. It is also probable that he may be to some degree crippled in his personal relationships as an adult if the tendency continues un-checked.

There is, it would seem, a simple and obvious way to avoid both *possible* schizoid developments and *possible* laming of the personality through habitual feelings of social inadequacy. This way is to provide the child with the deep sureness that comes out of the repeated experience of knowing that he is wanted, liked, respected and valued; that he "counts" and "belongs" and is im-portant. To provide such experience is good training, as David Klein says, because it may not only prevent mental illness but will increase the child's happiness in everyday living. It will, of course, serve the same end to teach him to plan and act realisti-cally instead of finding his gratifications in fantasy, and to take his failures without loss of confidence. All these things "are good because, if successful, they will bolster morale and contribute to the joy of living. If . . . they will also prevent functional men-tal disease, so much the better." [3]

The effort to build security in childhood may not always prevent mental illness, but it will prevent much mental illness, and it will never be wasted.

notes

Introduction

1. Sullivan, H. S.: *Conceptions of Modern Psychiatry.* Washington, D. C.: W. A. White Psychiatric Foundation, 1946, p. 7.
2. Menninger, W.: *Psychiatry in a Troubled World.* New York: Macmillan, 1948, p. 457.

Chapter 3

1. Cameron, N.: *Psychology of the Behavior Disorders.* Boston: Houghton Mifflin Co., 1947, p. 113.

Chapter 5

1. Freud, S.: *Collected Papers.* London: The Hogarth Press and the Institute of Psychoanalysis, 1953, Vol. II, p. 150 *et seq.*
2. Cameron, N.: *Psychology of the Behavior Disorders.* Boston: Houghton Mifflin Co., 1947, pp. 433-36.
3. *Ibid.,* p. 434.
4. Kafka, F.: *The Trial.* New York: Alfred A. Knopf, 1953.
5. ————: *Dearest Father: Stories and Other Writings.* New York: Schocken Books, 1954.
6. ————: *The Diaries of Franz Kafka: 1914-1923.* New York: Schocken Books, 1949, p. 213.
7. ————: *The Castle.* New York: Alfred A. Knopf, 1954.
8. ————: *Selected Short Stories of Franz Kafka.* New York: Random House, 1952.

Chapter 6

1. Schreber, D.: *Memoirs of My Nervous Illness.* Cambridge, Mass.: R. Bentley & Co. (Translated and edited by I. Macalpine and A. Hunter).

Chapter 7

1. Arieti, S.: *The Interpretation of Schizophrenia.* New York: Robert Brunner, 1955.
2. Hart, B.: *The Psychology of Insanity.* New York: The Macmillan Co., 1937, pp. 134-35.
3. Baldick, R.: *The Life of J.-K. Huysmans.* Oxford: The Clarendon Press, 1955, pp. 170-71.

4. Wells, H. G.: *Short History of the World*. London: Watts & Co., 1929, p. 47.
5. La Barre, W.: *The Human Animal*. Chicago: University of Chicago Press, 1954, p. 250.

Chapter 8

1. Storch, A.: *The Primitive Archaic Forms of Inner Experience and Thought in Schizophrenia*. New York: Nervous and Mental Disease Publishing Co., 1924, p. 97.
2. Strindberg, A.: *The Son of a Servant*. London: Wm. Rider & Sons, Ltd., p. 4.
3. ————: *The Inferno*. London: Wm. Rider & Sons, Ltd., 1912.

Chapter 9

1. Cameron, N.: "Experimental Analysis of Schizophrenic Thinking" in Kasanin, J. (ed.): *Language and Thought in Schizophrenia*. Berkeley and Los Angeles: University of California Press, 1951, p. 50.
2. *Ibid.*, p. 54.
3. *Ibid.*, p. 54.
4. Kasanin, J. S. (ed.): *Language and Thought in Schizophrenia*. Berkeley and Los Angeles: University of California Press, 1951, p. 130.
5. Cameron, N., *op. cit.*, p. 56.
6. Kasanin, J. S., *op. cit.*, pp. 129-30.
7. Arieti, S.: *The Interpretation of Schizophrenia*. New York: Robert Brunner, 1955, p. 195.
8. Kasanin, J. S., *op. cit.*, p. 129.

Chapter 10

1. White, R. W.: *The Abnormal Personality*. New York: Ronald Press, 1956, pp. 82-91.
2. *Ibid.*, p. 557.
3. Hill, L. B.: *Psychotherapeutic Intervention in Schizophrenia*. Chicago: University of Chicago Press, 1955, pp. 29-30.
4. *Ibid.*, p. 111.
5. May, E.: *The Meaning of Anxiety*. New York: The Ronald Press, 1950, p. 345.

Chapter 11

1. Klein, D. B.: *Mental Hygiene*. New York: Henry Holt & Co., 1956, p. 256.
2. *Ibid.*, p. 244.
3. *Ibid.*, p. 271.

index